WE LIKE IKE

WE LIKE IKE

THE EISENHOWER PRESIDENCY
AND 1950s AMERICA

ORGANIZED BY

J. RICHARD GRUBER

WITH

DENNIS MEDINA

This catalog is supported by the Friends of the Wichita Art Museum Alliance Holidays at the Wichita Art Museum Committee

CONTENTS

ACKNOWLEDGEMENTS

THE WE LIKE IKE EXHIBITION AT THE WICHITA ART MUSEUM GREW out of the desire to celebrate the 100th anniversary of the birth of Dwight David Eisenhower. It started with plans for a traveling exhibition of Eisenhower's paintings through the Kansas Traveling Visual Arts Program, based at the Wichita Art Museum with the support of the Kansas Arts Commission. As we continued to work with Eisenhower Library Curator Dennis Medina in Abilene, Kansas, we became more immersed in Eisenhower's life and in the important role Ike played in life in the 1950s and, as a result, in our lives today. Thus, the original exhibition of 16 paintings by Eisenhower evolved into this exhibition and catalog — a more detailed examination of the Eisenhower Presidency and 1950s America.

Neither the catalog or exhibition would have been possible without the commitment and support of the Friends of the Wichita Art Museum. The Mayor and City Council, Wichita Art Museum Board and the City of Wichita have all contributed to the success of this project. We gratefully acknowledge the contributions of time, expertise and finances from individuals, businesses and foundations which have resulted in We Like Ike.

The Wichita Art Museum particularly acknowledges:

The staff of the Dwight David Eisenhower Library: Museum Curator Dennis Medina for his curatorial expertise, his enthusiasm and his in-depth knowledge and respect for Dwight Eisenhower; Richard Norton Smith, Acting Director of the Eisenhower Library, for his insightful essay and support; Marion Kamm, who spent countless hours on the planning and organization of We Like Ike; Hazel Stroda for the photographic and archival research and support.

George Sexton and Evi Oehler of George Sexton Associates for the innovative design of the installation, which helps visitors understand Ike The Man, Ike The President and 1950s America; Polly Sexton for the design and layout of the catalog and graphics for the exhibition.

The staff of the Wichita Art Museum, particularly Dr. Novelene Ross, Carolyn Kell, Sharon White, Douglas King, Carole Branda, Leslie Servantez, Anita Walker and Henry Nelson. Special thanks to George Vollmer.

Ron Parks, Executive Director of the Kansas Eisenhower Centennial Commission.

We Like Ike

THE SURPRISING MR. EISENHOWER

"It is fatuous to remark that a man's hometown has changed since he was a boy. But in later visits to Abilene, I cannot help but notice that the nights, once so quiet that the whistle and rumble of a train could be heard rising and falling away across miles of country, are now disturbed by town noises. Something is missing. What is it?

Well, of course, it is my family. We are gone. Scattered, and we can never put the pieces together again."

Dwight D. Eisenhower
"At Ease"

WHEN DWIGHT EISENHOWER WROTE THOSE ELEGIAC WORDS NOT long before his death, he conveyed much more than a nostalgic longing for a simpler, less mechanized, less *pressing* era. In his own way, he was expressing the past's powerful hold on all of us. Near the end of his journey, a fabulous passage from hitching post to space capsule, the man from Abilene sought a frame of reference, a reminder of his origins and a gauge of just how far he had traveled since a childhood bounded by Mud Creek and the stark certainties of rural Kansas.

Throughout his Centennial year, Americans will remember the public Eisenhower—the architect of NATO and SEATO, the guiding spirit behind Operation Overlord and Atoms for Peace, the central figure in the headlines surrounding Little Rock and Omaha Beach and the flight of the U-2. Inevitably, however, many of us will recall the Age of Eisenhower with the same gauzy sentiments that Ike himself reserved for the Abilene of his youth. What railroad trains and livery stables were for him, Lucy and Elvis, 3-D movies and white buck shoes are for us.

Not to mention Eisenhower himself: an icon of the decade poised between the grim Thirties and wartorn Forties, and the turbulent generation that lost its leaders to assassination and lost its way in the jungles of Viet Nam. Is it any wonder that we harbor special feelings for the Kansas farmboy whose smile was as wide as the prairie? At the time, few suspected the rare political gifts that lay behind the smile. Only much later did historians and journalists come to agree with Richard Nixon, who wrote in *Six*

Preceding page: Inauguration Day, January 1953.
Right: Eisenhower at the first televised news conference.

Crises, "He was a far more complex and devious man than most people realized, and in the best sense of those words" Sherman Adams, whose 1958 ouster as White House chief of staff was instigated by the president but carried out by others, had his own assessment of Eisenhower, the supposed political innocent:

"He told Nixon and others, including myself, that he was well aware that somebody had to do the hard-hitting infighting, and he had no objections to it as long as no-one expected *him* to do it."

Eisenhower was a better fighter than infighter, as he demonstrated in North Africa and France. His was a genius for reconciliation, for melding disparate personalities and viewpoints into relative harmony. Anyone who could get along reasonably well with the likes of Bernard Montgomery, Charles DeGaulle, Winston Churchill, and Franklin Rooseveltnone of them exactly shrinking violetspossessed a unique gift for leadership.

It wasn't military theatre of the kind personified by Eisenhower's old drama coach, Douglas MacArthur, or the blood and guts persona of a Patton. Little that he said was memorable; he conjured no spells like FDR, and his speeches were devoid of young John Kennedy's trumpet calls to sacrifice. Yet Ike used words with far more skill than he was credited, sometimes to surprising effect. During his presidency, when tensions over the Formosa Strait were at their height, press secretary Jim Hagerty urged caution. Better to refuse any reporter's question about the world's number one trouble spot, urged Hagerty, than risk a crisis over U. S. policy toward what was then known as Red China.

Eisenhower had his own formula for such appearances, perfected over many years of what one perceptive student of his presidency has called "hidden hand leadership." Said Ike as he walked out the door to the White House press room, "Don't worry, Jim. If that question comes up, I'll just confuse them."

So subtle was Eisenhower's method, so complete the ruse, that Murray Kempton in describing it had recourse to the nonsense rhymes of Edward Lear:

"On the top of the Crumpetty Tree
The Quangle Wangle sat,
But his face you could not see,
On account of his Beaver hat.
For his hat was a hundred and two feet wide,
With ribbons and bippons on every side,
And bells, and buttons, and loops, and lace,
So that nobody ever could see the face
Of the Quangle Wangle Quee."

"Innocence," added Kempton, "was Eisenhower's beaver hat, and the ribbons grew longer and more numerous until his true lines were almost invisible. It took a very long time indeed to catch the smallest glimpse."

In titling his piece "The Underestimation of Dwight D. Eisenhower," Kempton anticipated the revisionist findings which, aided by unflattering memories of subsequent chief executives, have boosted Eisenhower into the ranks of America's most highly successful presidents. This alone is enough for many to harbor warm feelings toward the familiar figure in tan polo coat and brown snap brim hat, who steered a course between political extremes and applied in peace the lessons learned at such cost on the battlefield.

There are other, highly practical reasons to explain popular regard for the Fifties as a charmed decade. As has often been pointed out, it was a time of affluence as well as anxiety, when the threat of nuclear annihilation (and atomic mutants in the form of deadly spiders, moths, and other creatures threatening cities from Tokyo to Cleveland in the era's sci-fi movies) was outweighed by record prosperity. In 1954, the New York Stock Exchange at last regained its pre-1929 crash level of 381. Two years later, in the year of Eisenhower's triumphant re-election, 81% of his countrymen could watch Uncle Miltie, Ed Murrow, and Playhouse 90 on their own television sets. 96% of us owned refrigerators, 89% washing machines, 67% vacuum cleaners. Amid such widely dispersed wealth, it was easy to forget that at decade's end, forty million Americans lived below federally established subsistence levels $3,000 for a family of four, $4,000 for a family of six.

Other changes masked revolutionary currents flowing beneath the era's placid surface. The Eisenhower Administration completed Harry Truman's desegregation of the armed forces. Attorney General Herbert Brownell filed an amicus curiae (friend of the court) brief in Brown vs. Topeka Board of Education, the landmark case that dissolved legally mandated segregation in seventeen southern states, giving impetus to the civil rights revolution whose true leaders were Rosa Parks and a young Montgomery minister named Martin Luther King. And when Arkansas Governor Orval Faubus challenged the supremacy of the federal judiciary, Eisenhower responded by sending troops to escort the Little Rock Nine to class at Central High, where the ancient doctrine of "separate, but equal" no longer prevailed.

On both ends of the ideological spectrum, new protagonists appeared to argue their case: William F. Buckley launched National Review in 1955; C. Wright Mills lashed out about the same time at "power elites" who mocked the democratic premise and the Puritan ethic simultaneously. Sociologist David Riesman unveiled the "other directed man," conformist, urbanized, bureaucratized and materialistic. Academics fretting over the impact of progressive education pointed to a grapefruit-sized Russian satellite named Sputnik as a spur to U.S. science and technology.

The baby boom swelled America's population by twenty-nine million in a single decade. As important as the raw statistics of growth were the shifts occurring: from city to suburb, from northeast to southwest, from union hall to corporate office. The same year voters in record numbers endorsed Eisenhower for a second term over the wry, erudite Adlai Stevenson, America's working population for the first time ever contained more white collars then blue collars.

Amid so much that was impermanent, Ike became more than ever a symbol of continuity, of old values to be clung to in an age of accelerating change. The president's critics lampooned his gray pinstripe Cabinet as a millionaire's club, but to little avail.

After all, Ike's milieu was the very heart of America, in a town of few distinctions, whose capitalists spent much of their time currying horses and greasing buggy axles. Wall Street might gyrate like a kite in an April breeze, but the president remembered Cecil Brooks, telegraph operator in what Abilenians called a bucket shop, reputed to earn the fabulous salary of $125 a month, and warmly admired for his habit of keeping the wire to the East open each night during the World Series, the scores of which were promptly posted in a nearby poolroom.

Americans were bound to like a president who shared their cultural tastes, from Zane Grey novels to Clair de lune and who sat through "Around the World in 80 Days" four times. Let sophisticates debate the murky merits of Jackson Pollock and Mark RothkoIke stoutly refused to call his own artistic expressions by the name of paintings. "They are daubs," he confessed, "born of my love of color and in my pleasure in experimenting, nothing else." The president's only complaint about painting as a pastime was that it supplied no exercise. "I've often thought what a wonderful thing it would be to install a compact painting outfit in a golf cart."

In the republic of letters, Ike was a figure of derision. Most presidents are. He probably paid less attention to Tennessee Williams and Norman Mailer than they did to him. But he cherished a volume of poetry dropped off at the White House one day by Robert Frost, who wrote at the end of his inscription, "The strong are saying nothing until they see."

Frost saw what few others said. Ike could be a surprising figure. As president of Columbia University during the red-baiting days of 1949, the five star General of the Army dismissed the complaints of rich friends who saw Reds in every classroom. There would be no "intellectual iron curtain" at Columbia, he declared in permitting the teaching of Communist theory. At the same time, he founded a pioneering Institute of War and Peace Studies, launched a new Engineering Center and proved a genius at raising money with which to pad faculty salaries and the university endowment.

"It has been my invariable practice to refuse any honorarium," he informed a state education association eager to have him on its dais, and willing to pay $1,000 for the privilege, "and I shall most certainly adhere to that policy as long as I occupy any type of public office."

Eisenhower's recipe for vegetable soup—enhanced by nasturtium stems—received as much attention as any Commencement Day address he gave. Like most Americans, he was a zestful consumer.

"For me," he once explained, "a supermarket is an oriental bazaar. It is a wonderland of bargains, of foods I *must* try, of specialties I cannot pass by. This may be a reaction to the guarded and sparsely stocked shelves of my boyhood."

There it was again. Always he came back to Abilene. In old age, he recalled his hometown, once Cow Capital of the World, its Texas Street "a glowing thoroughfare which led from the dreariness of the open prairies into the delight of hell itself," as a marvelous playground for boys interested in fishing, baseball, football or boxing. Everyone went to church except those dubbed "poolroom sharks." Nearly everyone voted the Republican ticket.

Such a community afforded many opportunities for education. When he was ten years old and denied the right to accompany two older brothers one Halloween night, Dwight lost all control, pounding his fists bloody against an old apple tree in the yard of his parents' home. His father, a traditionalist in such matters, took a hickory switch to the boy and sent him to his room. After a while, his mother entered. She sat in a rocking chair for a long while, saying nothing. Then she began to paraphrase the Bible, talking of the need to master one's temper.

"He that conquereth his own soul is greater than he who taketh a city," she said.

Dwight Eisenhower never forgot those words, or the lesson they imparted. Nineteen times after the end of World War II, the victorious general who had taken many cities returned to a small town on the Smoky Hill River in Dickinson County, Kansas. After 1946, his customary practice was to pause before his mother's grave in the cemetery north of town. This year, hundreds of thousands of Eisenhower admirers will retrace his steps. For others, he will be just a name in a history book, a nostalgic figure used to sell cars or coins or golden oldies.

What will we tell them? Many things, really. We will tell them that once a seemingly ordinary Kansas family produced an extraordinary soldier and statesman. That because Ida Stover Eisenhower's son boarded a train east in the summer of 1911, because he wore the uniform of his country and led three million men in a daring assault on Fortress Europe; because of all this and much more, much of our world is free to think, to worship, to work and to vote as conscience directs.

A library, like a museum, serves many functions. It gathers the wisdom of the ages; it provides the diversion of a summer afternoon. But if such institutions have a single, overriding purpose, it is to connect us with the people and places, the ideas and experiences that enrich our lives and designate us guardians of a common heritage. At their best, libraries and museums foster connections: between neighbors and nations, between worlds that have been and worlds yet to be.

All this year, the Eisenhower Center, like the Wichita Art Museum through "We Like Ike" exhibit, will be connecting visitors to that faraway land we call the past. We will remind them of what it must have been like to live at 201 Southeast Fourth Street at the turn of the century, one of six boys in a two-story house, with a cherished piano in the front parlor and a backyard full of chickens, pigs, and rabbits. More important than the apples and pears raised by David and Ida Eisenhower on their three-acre lot were the boys grown there. They took root in the rich black earth of Dickinson County; they grew to embody the American Dream.

Said the adult Dwight Eisenhower of his boyhood home, "it provided both a healthy outdoor existence and a need to work...The same conditions were responsible for...a society which, more nearly than any other I have encountered, eliminated prejudices based upon wealth, race or creed."

Ike celebrated Abilene as an extended family: a classroom in self-sufficiency, taught by parents who paid their bills and neighbors who respected them for it. Abilene was a leveling ground, where bloodlines counted for little, and bank accounts for less. It was daily prayers and a swimming hole and football practice and brothers who sometimes carried their competition to scuffling in the yard. It was a place to learn in books what might later be applied in battles.

Dwight Eisenhower grew to maturity on a crowded stage, set against a backdrop of sunflowers and cottonwoods and the lonely majesty of the prairie, broken only by the occasional farm house or grain elevator. At night a blanket of stars covered the land, casting a glow unknown to city dwellers. With a boy's imagination, it was easy to picture a herd of Texas longhorns headed north, or Wild Bill Hickok striding down Buckeye Street larger than life.

Abilene taught and Abilene tested. Most of all, though, it instilled character. "I have found out in later years we were very poor," said Dwight Eisenhower when he came back to lay the cornerstone of a museum bearing his family's name, "but the glory of America is that we didn't know it then. All that we knew was that our parents—of great courage—could say to us: Opportunity is all about you. Reach out and take it."

Opportunity is what Eisenhower had in mind when he stood in London's ancient Guildhall in the spring of 1945 and declared, "I come from the very heart of America." Opportunity traveled with him when he returned to his roots two weeks later and said, "the proudest thing I can claim is that I am from Abilene." And opportunity was a fitting epitaph for the five-star general of the army who made his final homecoming in an $80 regulation casket, to lie in a plain stone chapel on the edge of the Kansas prairie.

It is easy to see why he came back.

Richard Norton Smith
Acting Director of the Dwight David Eisenhower Library,
Abilene, Kansas

IKE: THE BEGINNINGS

The Eisenhower family home, 201 Southeast Fourth Street, Abilene, Kansas.

Front Parlor

Middle Parlor

Middle Parlor

Kitchen

Dining Room

Parents Bedroom

Parents Bedroom

Upstairs Bedrooms

Sampler in Ike's Bedroom

Upstairs Bedroom (Ike's room)

THE ICONOGRAPHY OF "WE LIKE IKE"

"The popularity of President Eisenhower has got beyond the bounds of reasonable calculation and will have to be put down as a national phenomenon, like baseball. The thing is no longer just a remarkable political fact but a kind of national love affair. ..."
James Reston
The New York Times, September, 1955

"When he was president, most Americans cherished the national hero reigning benignly in the White House, a wise, warm, avuncular man who smiled a lot and kept the country calm and safe."
Arthur Schlesinger, Jr.
Look, May, 1979

"WE LIKE IKE" WAS FAR MORE THAN A SUCCESSFUL CAMPAIGN SLO-gan created by Eisenhower campaign strategists for the 1952 presidential campaign. By the middle of the decade, as the 1956 election approached, it was not surprising that the phrase evolved into "We Still Like Ike." Eisenhower's landslide '56 victory confirmed politically prevailing popular sentiment. Ike had become one of the most popular presidents in the nation's history. He had been a national hero since 1945. In fact, as James Reston suggested in the fall of 1955, the popularity of the president had become a "national phenomenon" which transcended politics, becoming "a kind of national love affair."

Americans' fascination with the Eisenhower presidency, and its manifestation in the art and popular culture of the time is the subject of this exhibition, "We Like Ike." Working in association with the Eisenhower Library, the Wichita Art Museum set out to explore the aesthetic and cultural interpretations of the "national love affair" between the president and people. However, as we soon discovered and as is evident in the range of objects included, the stature of Ike and Mamie was more than an American phenomenon; it was an international affair.

Left: Dwight and Mamie Eisenhower on their 40th wedding anniversary, July 1, 1956. Mamie is wearing dress of Blair House fabric.

In a decade when American values and popular culture exerted unprecedented international influence, it was no coincidence that Ike, America and the abundance of our material culture became so remarkably interwoven. America in the 1950s was an enormous, complex, wealthy and booming world power. After generations of cultural inferiority, America no longer apologized to the European nations and cultures from which it had been spawned. To Britain and the rest of the Western world, America was no longer a colony. The United States had become a full partner, in most areas a world leader. The American general who led the Allied forces to victory in World War II, the man who commonly was credited with saving European civilization from possible imminent destruction, was the same man who served as president through the years of peace and prosperity which marked 1950s America. Was it surprising that the nation and much of the western world developed such profound respect for Dwight David Eisenhower? In such an environment, wasn't it natural that Ike and Mamie became symbols, icons, of booming America in the years after World War II and prior to the beginning of the "New Frontier" and the tumultuous 1960s?

It was in the popular realm, not in the rarified environments of highbrows and "eggheads" that Ike's popularity and political success were so evident. Ike's ability to inspire the popular imagination and his own apparent lack of pretense about his role as an "average" American, one who came "from the very heart of America," were essential ingredients in the success of his presidency. In considering the evolution of his popularity and his image, this exhibition considers first his early years in Abilene and the West, then four major aspects of the Eisenhower fifties. They are: "Ike: The Campaigner"; "Ike: The President"; "Ike: At Ease"; and "Ike: The President and American Popular Culture."

IKE: ABILENE AND THE WEST

The public image of Dwight D. Eisenhower has undergone a series of profound changes since he left office. Revisionist historians continue to uncover a politician who was more complex, more subtle and more challenging than earlier interpretations suggested. As Richard Norton Smith indicates in his accompanying essay, Ike's association with Abilene and "heartland" American values was woven throughout the fabric of his political career. To understand Eisenhower, as man and politician, his sense of the importance of Abilene and the West must be considered. In 1958, Marquis Childs published an early "critical study" of the Eisenhower administration titled *Eisenhower: Captive Hero*. Childs observed that "perhaps more than anything else, Abilene may have shaped his character and purpose." In fact, Childs concluded: "Abilene was so right that no novelist would have ventured to put him there. Abilene: a small town, set only a few miles from the geographic heart of America...a town to be identified with America's most enduring native qualities." [1]

Eisenhower lived his first decades in the shadows of the great cattle drives, the gunfighters, outlaws and mythic lawmen. In his 1967 autobiography, *At Ease: Stories I Tell To Friends*, Eisenhower spoke of the reputation of Abilene in its early days: "It was then called the Cow Capital of the World. For a time it maintained its reputation as the toughest, meanest, most murderous town of the territory." [2] Born in Denison,

Texas, on October 14, 1890, he moved with his family to Abilene in 1891. He lived there, graduating from Abilene High School in 1909, until he departed for the U.S. Military Academy at West Point in June of 1911.

The home he left in 1911 was modest, even by prairie standards. The two-story white frame house was located on three acres of land. Here the family raised milk cows, ducks, pigs, chickens and rabbits; Eisenhower's parents gave each son a small garden plot, where vegetables could be grown for sale.[3] Inside, the series of small rooms, marked by austerity and limited color sensibility, suggests the humble beginnings of the man who would occupy the White House. The home was, and still remains, a distinctly nineteenth century environment. There is something mythical about the nature of this structure; it embodies the spirit of Horatio Alger and reminds the modern visitor of the humble beginnings of other presidents, including the "log cabin presidents" of the early nineteenth century. In 1926, when all Eisenhower sons returned for a family reunion, the family snapped a remarkable group photograph. Seated on the stairs of 201 South East Fourth Street, surrounded by parents and brothers, Major

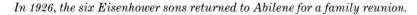

In 1926, the six Eisenhower sons returned to Abilene for a family reunion.

Dwight and Mamie in San Antonio, 1916.

Dwight Eisenhower, wearing a crisp uniform and handsome cavalry boots, looks confident and very much at home. Throughout his military and political career, as he returned to Abilene for family visits and campaign events, the stature of this house grew. It became part of the Eisenhower mystique.

After graduating from West Point in June of 1915, he returned to the state of his birth, where he was stationed at Fort Sam Houston, in San Antonio. There he met a stylish young visitor from Denver, Mamie Geneva Doud. Prior to their marriage in 1916, Eisenhower applied for service with the American Punitive Expedition, charged with the capture of the notorious Pancho Villa. Although he was not appointed to the unit, the exploits of Pancho Villa and his troops may have reminded Ike of the frontier adventures of the recent past. After their marriage in Denver, Ike and Mamie returned to live at Fort Sam Houston, where unsettling conditions continued to exist along the nearby border. Fearing for the safety of Mamie in his absence, Ike seemed to borrow a page from a western novel. He taught his young bride how to shoot a gun: "I gave her a .45 pistol and showed her, carefully, how to use it....She took it all seriously."[4]

Experiences from his early years must have stirred Eisenhower's considerable interest in the history and mythology of the American West. An avid reader and student of history, Eisenhower certainly recognized that his life paralleled the closing of the frontier as well as the progressive march from the early days of the automobile, to the atomic age and the beginnings of the space race. In his youth, the cult of the West was being preserved in a variety of ways. In 1902, during the year of Ike's twelfth birthday, Owen Wister published his famous book, *The Virginian,* and the first filmed western, *The Great Train Robbery,* was released. And, in the same year, popular novelist Benjamin Franklin Norris commented upon the loss of the frontier: "We liked the Frontier...it was romance, the place of poetry, of the Great March, the firing line where there was action and fighting, and where men held each other's lives in the crook of the forefinger."[5]

Ike was raised, in time and place, along the fringes of the last American frontier, along "the firing line." In the 1870s, Abilene was the railhead for the Chisholm Trail, cattle and cowboys filled the streets; Wild Bill Hickok had served as a marshall there. By the time he matured, in the twentieth century, that literal frontier environment was long gone. However, he discovered other frontiers, challenging modern frontiers which were beyond the imaginings of pulp novelists and western historians at the turn of the century. By the 1940s, he would experience perhaps the ultimate firing line. As Supreme Allied Commander, his responsibilities, including the strategic use of massive armies and new destructive technologies, far exceeded those of any mythic western hero. In the 1950s, when he resided in the White House, the soldier from Abilene kept the country at peace. It was one of his greatest accomplishments. Because the nation's economy and energy were not dissipated on warfare and military production, Americans were able to establish unprecedented material prosperity.

As president, he witnessed the popular revival of interest in the West. Western sagas appeared with increasing regularity on television and in movie theaters; a new generation of American youth, "the baby boom" generation, became fans of some of the same heroes and myths of his own childhood. And, like millions of other Americans, Ike and Mamie might be found watching television during free hours. Among the television westerns available to them were "Wild Bill Hickok," "Annie Oakley," "The Life and Legend of Wyatt Earp," "Gunsmoke," "Have Gun-Will Travel," "Maverick," "Lawman," "Rawhide," "Bonanza" and "Bat Masterson."[6] (One of the most popular shows of the period, "Death Valley Days," later served as a vehicle for a future president, Ronald Reagan.) At the end of his day in the White House, it remained common practice for the president to turn to his favorite bedside reading, western fiction, especially novels written by Zane Grey.

IKE: THE CAMPAIGNER

The national and international respect for Eisenhower which materialized during World War II raised speculation about his possible future as a presidential candidate even before the war ended. Although Eisenhower rejected all notions of a possible candidacy, the May 7, 1945, conclusion of the war in Europe initiated the beginnings of his course toward the White House. By that date, as Stephen Ambrose has indicated, "Eisenhower was one of the three best-known men in the world, just behind Stalin and Churchill. He had become the symbol of the forces that had combined to defeat the Nazis, and of the hopes for a better world."[7] A man with such appeal naturally intrigued the leaders of both political parties in the United States. His lack of interest in political office only enhanced his attractiveness.

His popularity, and his political potential, were more than evident in London when he gave his famous Guildhall address on June 12, 1945. In this, and in speeches and appearances in the following months, he consistently linked himself and his values to

Abilene. In the Guildhall address he compared London and Abilene and stated, "I come from the very heart of America."[8] When he returned to America, he appeared before an estimated crowd of two million people in New York and said, "I'm just a Kansas farmer boy who did his duty."[9] When he returned to Abilene, he told the twenty thousand people who filled City Park: "Through this world it has been my fortune, or misfortune, to wander at considerable distances....Never has this town been outside my heart and memory."[10] During this triumphant return to his home, he was asked about a possible entry into politics. He responded, "In the strongest language you can command you can state that I have no political ambitions at all."[11]

By 1948, both the Republican and Democratic parties sought Eisenhower as a presidential candidate. On June 6th of that year, a Roper poll showed Eisenhower was the top choice of voters in both parties. Despite this popularity and the growing possibility of a Draft Eisenhower movement at the Democratic Convention, he announced that he "could not accept nomination for any public office or participate in any political contest."[12] Once again, he had turned his back on a political career. Instead, he decided to accept the position of president of Columbia University. From 1950 to 1952, he served as NATO Commander; during these years he was granted a leave of absence from his duties at Columbia.

The limited military and political leadership evident in America at the beginning of the 1950s caused Eisenhower great concern. Throughout 1951, his friends and political advisors, as well as representatives from both the Democratic and Republican parties, urged him to run for the presidency. The number of Ike Clubs grew. Always the good soldier, Eisenhower began to soften his resistance, indicating that if duty called, even at the presidential level, it might be difficult to refuse. Still, he remained reluctant. He even kept his political party affiliation ambiguous until the beginning of 1952. Finally, when convinced that there was a national mandate and that the only other viable candidates would be Harry Truman and Robert Taft, he agreed to respond to a Republican Party draft.

Concluding his duties with NATO, Eisenhower returned to America and became a serious candidate for the presidency. Naturally, Abilene would be an essential early stop in the campaign. On June 4, he delivered a major political address in Abilene. It was his first nationally televised speech as a politician. The next day, he held a significant press conference in Abilene. And, beginning on June 6, he began a series of intensive meetings with state delegations who traveled to meet with him in Abilene.[13] As happened throughout his career, Abilene served as the platform, the starting point for another milestone in his development.

A major factor in the 1952 presidential campaign, as in the rest of American life, was television. On June 4, when Eisenhower's Abilene speech was broadcast to homes throughout the nation, he must have recognized how dramatically the country had changed since the days of his youth in that remote outpost. With the advent of television, no location would ever again be as removed, as sheltered, as the Kansas town of his childhood. Politics, news, movies, variety shows, commercials, game shows and, yes, even an obscure Southern singer named Elvis Presley, would soon infiltrate the

Eisenhower's February 2, 1953 State of the Union address was the first to be telecast, ushering in the age of electronic politics.

living rooms of America through the medium of television. As the 1950s progressed, Ike became one of television's greatest fans.

The era of the modern political campaign, centered on television and the concept of "media image," began in 1952. In 1948, radio had been the most advanced broadcast medium. Using dramatic sketches, some inspired by popular recordings and lyrics, both parties spent a total of $1,297,500 on network radio broadcasting in 1948.[14] By 1952, the medium of dominance became television. The influence of advertising men and the costs of political campaigning skyrocketed. The G.O.P. spent $1.5 million, more than both parties had spent in 1948, on one national spot campaign for Eisenhower. By the end of the campaign, the Democrats spent $1.2 million for radio and television. The Republicans spent more than $2.5 million.[15]

In July of 1952, Eisenhower became the Republican nominee for the presidency in the first national convention covered by live TV. At the time of Eisenhower's first campaign, almost 44 million American homes contained at least one radio and over 19 million homes had a television set. (In 1956, when Ike campaigned for re-election, the number of televisions had grown to 36.7 million).[16] With television campaigns, the broadcast image of candidates became a critical issue. Adlai Stevenson, who resisted campaign "packaging," projected an "intellectual" image. Eisenhower, in spots created by the BBDO advertising agency, was presented as "the hero." For scheduled 30 minute speeches, BBDO structured 10 minutes of televised arrival and departure before enthusiastic crowds; the actual speeches lasted only 20 minutes.[17] Another element of the television campaign centered on Eisenhower question-answer messages, where the candidate became a controlled performer, giving concise and clear responses to the concerns of the nation.

Even the vice-presidential candidate used television to his advantage. In one of the most famous television campaign appearances, the "Checkers" speech, Richard Nixon defended his reputation and denied the illegal use of campaign funds for personal matters. With Pat Nixon carefully placed next to him during the broadcast, Nixon did admit keeping one campaign gift—"a little cocker spaniel dog in a crate" which his six-year old daughter Tricia had named "Checkers." In a direct plea to the families of America, he announced: "And you know the kids love that dog and I just want to say this right now, that regardless of what they say about it, we're going to keep it."[18] The popular support that resulted from this televised speech kept Nixon on the ticket as the vice-presidential candidate. Broadcast to over 67 TV stations and several hundred radio stations, the speech cost the Republican party $75,000.

In addition to the use of this new medium, the Eisenhower campaign relied on many more traditional campaign techniques and products. As is evident in this exhibition, the phrases "I Like Ike" and "We Like Ike" were applied to buttons, bumper stickers, hats, dresses, banners, ties, jewelry, umbrellas, cigarette packages, cups, sunglasses, and a wide range of other objects. Having demonstrated his ability to use the new medium of television, Eisenhower also mastered one of the older American campaign vehicles, the whistle-stop train tour. In September, Ike and Mamie conducted a wide-ranging and exhilarating train campaign which proved highly successful.[19]

On the evening of November 4, 1952, Ike and Mamie, like millions of other Americans, watched television to learn the results of the election. It was a resounding victory for Eisenhower who got 33,936,234 votes (55.1 percent) to Stevenson's 27,214,992 (44.4 percent). He received 442 electorial votes to Stevenson's 89 votes.[20] The tremendous popularity of Eisenhower, as a man and a politician, was the central issue in the 1952 campaign. Eight years later, Sidney Hyman, writing for *The New York Times*, explained that Ike's continuing popularity was a major factor in the impending outcome of the 1960 elections. Hyman identified three major elements in the popularity of Ike. First was the public's estimate of his "superior character," which "cast a golden glow over his presidential presence." Second was his experience: "Mr. Eisenhower...came to

*The victorious Eisenhowers at GOP headquarters, Hotel Commodore, New York,
November 4, 1952.*

the Presidency with his place in universal history already won. ... He was formed...on Europe's field of battle—a victorious Supreme Commander sent by heaven to be the savior of nations." He explained the "mystique" of Eisenhower by noting that here "if anywhere else in modern times, was a piece of Greek mythology came to life, this birth of a fully shaped hero." Finally, the "ambivalent American attitude toward power" made Ike an ideal president. Following World War II, the Korean War and the Cold War, Americans knew the value of military power but did not trust it. Ike, the experienced general, understood and used military power, yet he too seemed to have "a deep-seated distrust of power outside the battlefield." These three elements of the Eisenhower character contributed, Hyman concluded, to the "father-image," the "father-protector" quality, which so marked the Eisenhower presidency.[21]

IKE: THE PRESIDENT

Eisenhower wasted little time demonstrating his commitment to honor his campaign pledges. During the campaign he had promised to travel to Korea to study the political and military environment of the war zone. By the end of November, just weeks after the election, he boarded a plane for Korea. Early into his first year in office, Eisenhower halted the Korean War with a popular truce. He addressed a wide range of issues in his first years as president, but, as throughout the campaign and the later years of his administration, it was the person and personality of the president that had the greatest impact. In 1958, Marquis Childs studied the first Eisenhower administration and concluded, "He was enjoying life, and so were we all. This was why we elected Eisenhower: no American boy was being shot anywhere, our taxes had been cut, and we were on our way to making eight million automobiles in a single year."[22] In a later study of the Eisenhower years, Robert Wright confirmed that it was Eisenhower's "sheer presence, more than any of his policies, that soothed the nation's nerves." Continuing, he observed: "Having coordinated a global assault on evil, the man obviously knew a threat when he saw one; and yet he didn't look worried. There he was, golfing and grinning, as if he didn't have a care in the world. People calmed down."[23]

As president, Eisenhower clearly gave most Americans what they desired when they voted for him. While his critics might correctly identify his shortcomings, most voters had little problem with his style of management. Recent scholarship tells us there is much we still don't understand about the intricacies of the Eisenhower administration, yet it is quite evident that the general was a highly skilled politician who did much more than grin. Richard Smith's essay examined this issue. Historians

Following his election, Ike kept his campaign promise and went to Korea. Here he shares dinner with Sgt. Jack R. Hutcherson.

and critics agree that the years of the Eisenhower presidency were unique for the effects of peace and prosperity which were characteristic of the period. Of course, the average American living during the 1950s didn't need a scholar to explain that point. It was obvious. And it was equally obvious that Ike and Mamie personified the nation's mood through these years.

As the portraits included in this exhibition demonstrate, Ike and Mamie were favorite subjects for professional and amateur artists throughout the nation and the world. The "official" Eisenhower, the formally posed world leader, often seen with the popular first lady, is conspicuously present in paintings and portrait busts. With oil on canvas, pastels, in marble, bronze and plaster, Ike the President, as well as Ike the General and Supreme Allied Commander, was preserved for the ages. These images tell us much about the stature of Eisenhower, and they also serve as examples of the continuing traditions of portraiture during the years after 1950.

Equally interesting to the contemporary viewer are the numerous portraits submitted to a beloved leader by amateur artists from throughout the world. In addition to oil paintings and watercolors, these include wood carvings, black velvet paintings, a painted leaf, woven portraits, a collage constructed of postage stamps and a woven straw image from Mexico. The amateur portraits of Ike in this exhibition include a wide range of poses and costumes including: Ike as a cowboy on horseback; as a chef preparing chili; wearing a Mexican Charro outfit; as a four-star general portrayed in a wood inlay technique, and a painting on a corrugated surface which depicts Ike from one perspective and Adlai Stevenson from the opposite angle. The majority of paintings and objects reinforce the earlier campaign images and document the public's response to Eisenhower as a person and as a politician.

Throughout his presidency, Eisenhower worked hard to maintain his stature as a hero, as a figure above partisan politics and as a professional soldier who knew the

Ike was adulated by people around the world, who presented him with their images of him, such as this one from Mexico, complete with sombrero and serape.

Eisenhower turns on the power at the nation's first atomic power plant.

limitations and implications of nuclear warfare. In short, he worked hard to maintain his popular image as "Ike". This public image was carefully crafted and carefully maintained. This "Ike" persona was, to a large degree, a projection of his self image. For the majority of voters this image was reassuring throughout his presidency.

To many journalists, scholars and historians it was less than successful. In 1962, a poll of American political scientists and historians placed Eisenhower on the lower level of American presidents. Viewed as a listless and mediocre politician, a glorified duffer, he was ranked between Chester A. Arthur and Andrew Johnson.[24] A shift was evident in 1967 when Murray Kempton focused on Ike's political sophistication: "He was the great tortoise upon whose back the world sat for eight years. We laughed at him; we talked wistfully about moving; and all the while we never knew the cunning beneath the shell."[25] By the time of his death in 1969, and continuing through the era of the Ronald Reagan presidency, Eisenhower's political and critical reputations improved significantly.

In 1970, Richard Rhodes suggested in *Harper's Magazine* that "No one seems to have understood that he was a brilliant man." Rhodes deduced that his accomplishments "were those you would expect of a soldier and a son of small-town Kansas folk: the St. Lawrence Seaway, the Interstate Highway system, the National Defense Education Act, the nuclear submarine, the Polaris Missile." Greatest of all, he concluded, was that Eisenhower "gave us eight years of peace, with more provocation to war than was ever visited upon either John Kennedy or Lyndon Johnson."[26]

By 1979, Fred I. Greenstein completed a lengthy study of the Eisenhower presidency and announced: "Eisenhower was politically astute and informed, actively engaged in putting his personal stamp on public policy, and applying a carefully thought-out conception of leadership to the conduct of the presidency."[27] Arthur Schlesinger, Jr., a former critic of the Eisenhower presidency, found a degree of respect for him by 1979: "Far from being a political innocent, he was a politician of the first water....Far from being an amiable bumbler, he calculated his incoherence to conceal his purpose. Far from being an incompetent executive, he dominated his administration on all critical issues."[28] More concisely, a 1980 essay in *Time* magazine reflected the more cynical expectations among voters in the months prior to the election of Ronald Reagan: "Eisenhower's was the last complete presidency that began and ended without tragedy or trauma or disgrace."[29]

A more recent and thorough revisionist account of the Eisenhower presidency appeared in 1984 when Stephen Ambrose published *Eisenhower, The President*. Ambrose describes a president with extraordinary intellect, political skills and media savvy. He also described a remarkable person. When he entered office, Eisenhower was 62 years old, weighed 175 pounds, was of medium height (5 feet 10 inches), ate and drank in moderation, and, as his tanned complexion and brisk physical bearing suggested, he golfed and exercised regularly. As a person, he inspired confidence, and was commonly described as "trustworthy." His military experience prepared him well in foreign affairs and trained him in the inner workings of Washington politics. Despite his self-deprecating manner, his easy grin, and his seemingly relaxed air, he was used to being the center of attention and to having the power required to make major decisions.[30]

A typical working day for the president, as reconstructed by Ambrose, would have exhausted most younger men. He commonly rose around 6 a.m., dressed, and immersed himself in morning papers during breakfast. He read *The New York Times*, the *Herald Tribune* and the Washington papers. By 8 a.m. he was at his desk in the Oval office, where he worked until 1 p.m. After a working lunch, he continued in his duties until about 6 p.m. The evening meal seems to have interested him little. By 1952, he began eating dinner off a TV tray while absorbing the TV news. After dinner, he worked until about 11 p.m., his schedule of speeches and social events permitting. Finally, he put in an hour of painting before retiring. In bed, the day ended by reading western fiction.[31]

On November 6, 1956, voters elected Eisenhower to a second term as president. He again defeated opponent Adlai Stevenson, this time by an even wider margin than in the first campaign. The vote was 35,581,003 for Eisenhower and 25,738,765 for Stevenson.[32] After Eisenhower suffered a severe heart attack in the fall of 1955, many feared that he would not run for a second term. During his second campaign, he put the power of television to work. Due to his health, and his belief that a standing president should not demean the office by campaigning state to state, Eisenhower poured his energy and charm into producing television spots. Again, he used the BBDO agency. The $2.5 million Republican broadcast campaign included one minute "blitz" commercials, five minute spots trailing popular TV shows, and longer "The People Ask The

President" segments. Reluctantly, Stevenson hired his own advertising agency to attempt competitive commercials. Stevenson complained, "this idea that you can merchandise candidates like breakfast cereal—that you can gather votes like box-tops—is I think the ultimate indignity to the Democratic process."[33] Like it or not, television's political impact upon the Democratic process was established fact, and there would be no going back.

During his second term, Eisenhower achieved momentous program advances and encountered major challenges. Before the fall election, on June 29, 1956, he signed into law the National System of Interstate and Defense Highways. The impact of that legislation, as new automobiles filled with families crossed the nation in unprecedented numbers, was clearly evident throughout his second term. During these same years, the U-2 espionage plane began flights over the Soviet Union with Eisenhower's approval. In September of 1957 he ordered federal troops into Little Rock to enforce a Federal court order on segregation. The next month the Soviet Union fired Sputnik, the first man-made satellite, into orbit presenting a crisis for national confidence. At the beginning of 1958, the United States shot its own first satellite, Explorer I, into space; the space race was underway.

In the last two years of his administration, Eisenhower extended the frontiers of the nation and the presidency. He became the first president to travel by jet and by helicopter. He enthusiastically jetted to diverse foreign lands for serious diplomacy and to speak good will. Alaska, with its massive wilderness, and Hawaii, exotic and equally remote, achieved statehood under Ike's stewardship. Ike absorbed tales of the Western frontier during his childhood in Abilene. As he reached the end of his second term, he had circled the globe in an American jet, added two stars to the flag, and launched our space program. Ike had pushed into new frontiers during his presidency.

IKE: AT EASE

One of Eisenhower's greatest and most publicized skills as president was his ability to relax. Whether golfing, painting, fishing, hunting, playing bridge, traveling with Mamie or visiting with his grandchildren at the Gettysburg farm, the image of Ike enjoying his leisure time was ever present during the 1950s. To some critics, this suggested that he did not work hard enough at being president. Others recognized his example was essential. If the president relaxed, perhaps the nation could begin to relax. After the economic and social pain of the Great Depression, the trauma of World War II, and the continuing tensions of the Cold War and the Korean War, Americans were ready to devote more time to enjoying life. As the nation quickly learned, Ike took relaxation seriously. Following his example, Americans began to enjoy more and more expanded leisure pursuits. Having fun became big business.

During the 1950s, as America established itself as the world power in art, as Abstract Expressionist interests waned and Pop Art emerged, the president built a reputation as an amateur painter, perhaps in spite of himself. His paintings were far removed from the theories and styles of such Abstract Expressionists as Jackson Pollock, Barnett Newman, Franz Kline and Mark Rothko. Although he was interested

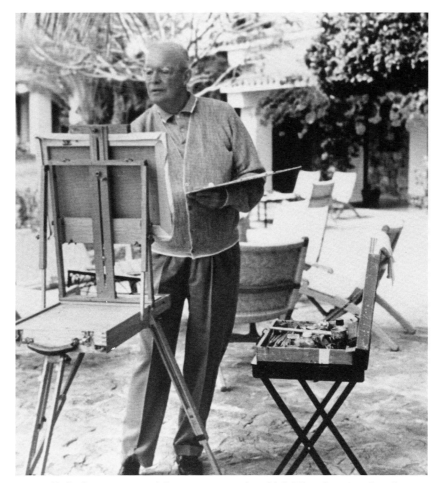

Painting was one of the many ways in which Eisenhower relaxed.

in realistic subject matter, he was little concerned with exploring the essence of American popular and material culture in the manner of Andy Warhol and his colleagues. Dwight Eisenhower was a self-proclaimed Sunday painter, a weekend dauber; he was a successful political leader and military hero who found painting enjoyable and relaxing. In style and imagery he was closer to Grandma Moses than to Andy Warhol. Like Winston Churchill, another world leader who was recognized as a painter, he found pleasure in painting and recognized its power to alleviate the pressures of his office.

In contrast to the complex aspirations and theories associated with many major painters of his day, Eisenhower's interest in painting was simple and simply explained. In 1967 he told a reporter, "There's nothing philosophical about my interest in painting. Rather, it is the best way in the world to relax. You put the surface of your mind on the canvas while the rest of your mind is making decisions."[34] Eisenhower favored the practical, direct approach in art. Reporting on his painting in April of 1960, a writer for the *Saturday Evening Post* concluded: "He paints simple, representational pictures. ...He is impatient with art that is the product of introspection rather than observation."[35] And, as he admitted late in his career, his technical skills were far from perfect: "After eighteen years, I am still messy; my hands are better suited to an ax handle than a tiny brush. I attempt only simple compositions....Even yet I refuse to refer to my productions as paintings."[36] Despite these limitations, the president loved to paint. During his White House years, he worked to maintain a regular schedule of painting at the end of the day, usually beginning at 11 p.m.. He even found it difficult to stay away from his paintings during the business day: "In the White House, in bad weather, painting was one way to survive away from the desk. In a little room off the elevator on the second floor, hardly more than a closet, the easel, paints, and canvases were easy to use. Often, going to lunch, I'd stop off for ten minutes to paint."[37]

Eisenhower turned to painting with the encouragement of Winston Churchill and with the support of Thomas Stephens. In 1948, after the Eisenhowers moved into the president's home at Columbia University, Stephens was commissioned to paint Mamie's portrait. Somewhat intimidated by the marble and architectural formality of their new residence on Morningside Drive, Ike and Mamie spent much time in a converted room on the roof which overlooked Harlem and the lights of Long Island. Here Stephens painted Mamie's portrait. As the portrait neared completion, Stephens and Mamie left the painting and the room to locate a spot for its installation. Left behind, Ike studied the portrait, obtained a simple canvas, and began to paint his own version of Mamie's portrait, using Stephens' palette and brush. When Stephens and Mamie returned, they were amazed. Stephens asked for, and Ike gave this first painting as a souvenir. Within a brief time, he sent Eisenhower a complete painting outfit. Using a tarp to cover the floor of his private penthouse retreat, Eisenhower soon experimented with the paints: "The one thing I could do well from the beginning was to cover hands, clothes, brush handles, chair and floor with more paint than ever reached the canvas. With the protection provided by the tarp...I succeeded in avoiding total domestic resistance to my new hobby."[38]

In his retreat at the president's residence at Columbia, and later in his isolated studio at the White House, Eisenhower focused on improving his craft. The majority of his paintings were portraits. Examples of his portraiture included in this exhibition depict such diverse subjects as Princess Anne and Floyd Odlum; a group composition features John Foster Dulles, George M. Humphrey and George E. Wilson. Eisenhower's respect for two earlier presidents is reflected in his portraits of George Washington and Abraham Lincoln. (In the Oval office, Ike was surrounded by formal portraits of the American leaders he most admired—Benjamin Franklin, George Washington, Abraham Lincoln and Robert E. Lee.[39]) In addition to portraits, he also focused much of his energy on landscapes. He often painted these scenes from photographs or magazine illustrations. When possible, as during his visits to his Gettysburg farm, he tried to paint outdoors. Landscapes included in this exhibition depict Alpine scenes, the Seine River, an unidentified waterfall, a snow-filled view of winter birches and an abandoned barn. He painted the Aspen Lodge at Camp David during one of his visits to the presidential retreat. And, of course, he painted his beloved Abilene home.

The exact number of Eisenhower paintings still in existence is unclear. Although he was ambitious in his painting, he felt the finished works were of little lasting value. He destroyed two out of each three paintings he began. Commonly, he gave the completed paintings to friends or guests as souvenirs. When a friend visited, Ike might paint while they conversed. In February of 1953, for example, Bill Robinson spent the weekend at the White House. During an afternoon, while Ike painted, he and Robinson carried on a spirited conversation: "He seldom sits in the same chair for very long during a discussion and abhors sitting behind a desk in any extended conference. During our two- or three-hour talk he was all over the room and he continued to talk animatedly while he worked on the painting."[40] Although his love of painting was widely publicized, Eisenhower refused to formally exhibit his work. The only exception to this came in 1967, when he allowed a group of paintings to be displayed in a New York gallery to promote a publication, *The Eisenhower College Collection, The Paintings of Dwight D. Eisenhower*. He endorsed this book and the related publishing of calendars and prints using his paintings to support Eisenhower College.

Eisenhower loved to totally immerse himself in painting and in his other hobbies. The concentration required in these pursuits offered an escape, a release from the constant pressures of his position. Stephen Ambrose has suggested that Ike's hobbies gave the president pleasure and "mental rejuvenation" which were sorely needed: "It was characteristic of Eisenhower that when he needed to escape his daily cares, he wanted to participate actively, not passively, in the escape....He could not 'lose' himself in a book, a concert, or a masterpiece, but he did 'lose' himself when he was on a trout stream, painting, playing golf or bridge."[41] He commonly enjoyed golf, bridge and fishing with a close group of successful friends, including Bill Robinson, Pete Jones, George Allen, Cliff Roberts and Ellis Slater.

During the White House years, Ike and Mamie escaped to their Gettysburg farm to relax with family and close friends as often as they could. Here Ike could paint, play bridge, golf and pursue the pleasures of a gentleman farmer. The Eisenhowers had purchased the Gettysburg farm as a home to enjoy during their retirement. Always the son of Abilene and the fertile Kansas farmlands, Ike intended it to be a working farm. Having grown up in one of the great cattle towns of the Old West, it was probably natural that the Eisenhower farm became a respected center for raising purebred Angus cattle. Soon after taking office, in the spring of 1953, Eisenhower and Ellis Slater discussed the possibility of Ike's assumption of duties as a full-time cattle rancher after he returned from the presidency in 1957. [42] After suffering a heart attack in September of 1955, Eisenhower spent six weeks recuperating in a Denver hospital. In November, he returned to Gettysburg where he began his full recovery. During this period he painted, read, watched the activities of his cattle and farm crews and enjoyed his private putting green. Here, too, he decided to seek re-election in the 1956 campaign. Throughout his career, Ike was able to put his work aside to enjoy his hobbies and his friends. These sojourns allowed him to become rejuvenated and recharged, and to return to his responsibilities with a new level of energy and creativity.

Above: The Eisenhowers with grandchildren Anne, Susan and David at Gettysburg farm.
Below left to right: Susan, Ike, Barbara, Anne, John, David and Mamie at Camp David.

IKE: THE PRESIDENT AND AMERICAN POPULAR CULTURE

When Ike campaigned in 1956, he used television and his successful media image to great advantage. By 1956, there were more than 36 million televisions in America. At the end of the nation's favorite television shows, viewers saw commercials for Eisenhower, reminding them who was responsible for the prosperity and peace they enjoyed. Images of Ike merged with these shows— "I Love Lucy," "The Ed Sullivan Show," "Gunsmoke," "The $64,000 Question," and "I've Got a Secret"— and became even more a part of the popular culture of America. That year, seventeen recordings of "The Ballad of Davy Crockett" were made; coonskin caps became popular. Inflation stood at 1.2%. Unemployment held steady at 4.3%. During the year 11% of all cars sold were station wagons. Thousands of young families travelled across the nation in new cars, visiting relatives, national parks, beaches and new tourist centers such as Disneyland. Americans viewed westerns, Hitchcock and Presley in more than 7,000 drive-in theatres.[43] The rush to the suburbs continued unabated. As the nation relaxed and more people enjoyed unprecedented levels of material comfort, Eisenhower sought re-election. There was little doubt about the outcome. Americans had many good reasons to still like Ike.

Ike and Mamie remained closely aligned with the values of mainstream America throughout the 1950s. As the "baby boom" generation continued to develop, family values dominated much of the national interest. Television was filled with programs devoted to nuclear families including "I Love Lucy," "Make Room for Daddy," "Father Knows Best," "Leave It to Beaver," and "The Donna Reed Show." Eisenhower's extended White House family filled news reports and popular magazines of the period. Ike and Mamie were proud grandparents who regularly displayed their beaming grandchildren to a national audience. In the era of the family backyard barbecue, Ike was known as an avid cook. While countless suburban fathers tended grills on their new patios, the nation's leader wore an apron and revealed his cooking secrets.

For most middle-class Americans, the 1950s seemed to be a time of unbounded opportunity. Most people lived more comfortably than in the past and spent fewer hours working. There was more time available to devote to families and to enjoy leisure activities. Fueled by easy credit, rampant consumerism became a hallmark of the period. New houses, sleek cars, fast boats, larger televisions, sophisticated hi-fi systems, modern appliances and countless gadgets lured the consumer of the 1950s. By the end of the decade, suburbs claimed one-fourth of the American population. Inspired by the tract houses and subdivisions of developers such as William Levitt and Henry J. Kaiser, new families enjoyed a standard of living not widely available to earlier generations. A qualified veteran could buy a new house with a modern kitchen and bedrooms for all the children for $6,990; payments were only $65 per month.[44]

The automobile became the ultimate consumer item in the 1950s. Growing ever larger and more luxurious as the decade evolved, sprouting tail fins as the jet age appeared, the automobile generated unbridled passions in the years of the Eisenhower administration. Ike's commitment to the development of a comprehensive Interstate Highway network, supported by the availability of inexpensive gasoline, prompted even greater growth in the automobile industry. New automobiles filled garages in

Mamie greets guests at a White House lawn party for senior citizens.

suburbia and lined parking lots at shopping centers. Families could drive to the new McDonald's restaurants and stop along the highway to spend the evening in a modern, air-conditioned Holiday Inn room (with no additional charge for the children). In 1956, there were an estimated seventy-five million cars and trucks on the nation's streets. [45] In addition to the Fords, Chevrolets, Corvettes, Thunderbirds, Edsels, Studebakers and Buicks available to the consumer of the late 1950s, there was also a growing selection of imported automobiles. In 1958, for example, when an Oldsmobile sold for $2,933, Renault offered a less expensive alternative sedan for $1,345.[46]

After acquiring a house and a car, the consumer of the Eisenhower era might spend leisure time in the many new supermarkets, department stores and shopping centers opening around the nation. Shopping, and the pursuit of ever more current fashions, became a major passion during the period. Mamie Eisenhower, known for her famous hairstyle and her extensive wardrobe, certainly reflected these national interests. And Ike's love of golf, painting, fishing and bridge certainly reflected the range of other leisure activities being explored. Additional national leisure trends included bowling, boating, amateur photography, hunting, gardening, wood working, crafts, weaving and "do-it-yourself" projects. Ike, the well-known golfer and painter, appeared to consider himself just another citizen enjoying his leisure time.

The advent of the jet age, and the availability of commercial jet travel, opened vast new parts of the world to American tourists. The American passenger jets of the late 1950s—the Boeing 707, the Convair 880 and the Douglas DC-8— embodied the spirit of the future and showcased the technological superiority of the nation's engineering and manufacturing giants. These planes suggested speed, unlimited opportunities and the international influence of American corporations. Dwight Eisenhower, the product of 19th century Abilene, became the first president to fly in a jet. In 1959 and 1960, the Eisenhowers circled the globe in the presidential jet, visiting exotic locations and carrying the good will of America to diverse nations. A number of the portraits included in this exhibition were completed by artists in these remote countries in response to the symbolic visits of the Eisenhowers. Like other Americans who traveled, Ike became an amateur photographer; increasingly, his camera became a regular item on these trips.

Large portions of the growing teen culture matured during the Eisenhower years. Teenagers became a vital segment of the consumer economy of the 1950s. Appealing to these teen markets became big business. A 1957 article in *Newsweek* chronicled spending patterns of the nation's teenagers and reported that they had disposable income of $9 billion in that year.[47] Recognizing the potential influence of this audience, Eisenhower's campaign managers focused special attention on this youth culture in 1956. The poodle skirt, embroidered with Ike imagery and the "Peaceniks for Ike" logo, included in this exhibition, reflects this focus on the nation's teenagers. Increasingly, however, teenagers of the 1950s were finding younger role models.

When Eisenhower campaigned for re-election in 1956, a wide new range of teenage idols had emerged. One of the first appeared in 1954 when Marlon Brando, wearing jeans and a leather jacket, rode a motorcycle to fame in "The Wild One." Changing tastes in music became evident that same year when Alan Freed, a disc jockey for radio station WINS, introduced a type of music he called "rock 'n roll." By 1955, actor James Dean achieved prominence by playing a sensitive youth who was misunderstood by

Eisenhower's 1956 campaign capitalized on the growing teen culture, with poodle skirts added to campaign materials.

parental figures in "Rebel Without a Cause" and "East of Eden." Another popular film, "The Blackboard Jungle," focused on a teenage gang responsible for disrupting the life of a high school. Equally popular was the movie's title song "Rock Around the Clock," by Bill Haley and His Comets; it became a national and international rock anthem. These and other young stars, including Natalie Wood, Sal Mineo, Marilyn Monroe, Little Richard, Chuck Berry and Fats Domino, embodied values far removed from those of Eisenhower's own youth.[48]

During the year of his second campaign, no celebrity embodied the spirit of this new youth culture more than Elvis Aron Presley. And no individual offered better evidence of the continuing durability of the American Dream than this modest and often deferential son of a truck driver, born into poverty in Tupelo, Mississippi, and who had matured in a Memphis public housing project. Recording with Sam Phillips' Sun

Eisenhower gave the 1960 Republican presidential ticket his support and influence.

Records label in Memphis in 1954 and 1955, he rose to regional stature in the South. On January 16, 1956, when he stepped into an RCA Records studio in Nashville to record "Heartbreak Hotel," he became a national leader of a different constituent. Before the year ended, he had recorded "Blue Suede Shoes," "Don't Be Cruel," "Hound Dog" and "Love Me Tender."[49] His sensational appearances on the Ed Sullivan program shocked parents and thrilled their children. These TV performances violated the sanctity of the nation's living rooms by bringing the undeniable presence of the rebellious youth culture directly into the home. Many older Americans were baffled by the screaming crowds who attended his concerts and by the throngs who flocked to his first movie, a western called "Love Me Tender." By the end of 1956, Presley joined the growing list of American millionaires. In spite of his image as a social rebel, Elvis developed a fondness for new Cadillacs. In 1957, he purchased Graceland Mansion in Memphis for over $100,000. By the time Eisenhower was sworn in for a second term as president, Elvis Presley was established as a revolutionary force in American music and a national icon for a new generation. He also became a direct beneficiary of the prosperity of the era. It all culminated in one pivotal year, 1956.[50]

THE ICONOGRAPHY OF "WE LIKE IKE"

Jack Kennedy and Dick Nixon faced a similar challenge as they campaigned for the presidency in 1960. For these two young candidates, the issue centered on the American voter's continuing approval of the policies of the Eisenhower administration. To the average American Ike remained as popular as ever. In fact, Ike was one of the few presidents who was more popular when he left office than when he entered. How could Kennedy or Nixon establish a unique identity, become a new political presence, without sacrificing those voters who still liked Ike? Now an elder statesman, Ike had kept the peace and delivered new prosperity directly to most voters. He had established himself and the nation as world leaders. During his presidency, Winston Churchill, Charles de Gaulle, Nikita Krushchev, Bernard Montgomery and other international figures paid official visits to Eisenhower. And, by his example, he encouraged the nation to relax, to enjoy its new stature. Americans achieved a new level of confidence during his presidency.

In 1960, as he completed his second term of office, Eisenhower reviewed the accomplishments of his administration. He took distinct pride in the prevailing environment of economic well-being and in the advances in the American standard of living. As proof of the nation's stability, he referred to specific economic indicators, comparing conditions in 1952 to 1960: average family income had increased by 15%; real wages had increased by 20%; the production of goods had grown by 25% and major advances were evident in both housing and school construction.[51] Inflation remained low and employment continued at high levels. His determined efforts had kept the nation's energies focused on productivity, not confrontation. Although they may not have studied the government's statistics, the majority of Americans recognized that they enjoyed a standard of living which exceeded that of any preceding generation. They knew they had Ike to thank for much of that prosperity.

Americans also recognized that the stature of the presidency had increased enormously during the Eisenhower years. For the average American in 1960, the image of the president inspired trust and new confidence in the nation's future. Eisenhower had played a role in American history and public service for years; from the beginning of World War II until 1961, when he left the White House, he flourished under the most exhaustive and intensive forms of public scrutiny. In the process of organizing and researching this exhibition, drawing from the extensive resources of the Eisenhower Library, it became apparent that a recurring system of symbols and motifs could be found in Eisenhower's archives and collections. His public image was, it seems, reinforced by a subtle, yet consistent program of visual signs and symbols which embodied elements of the history and myth of Ike.

There is, we discovered, an iconography of Ike. As this essay has suggested, there are themes and motifs evident through the range of objects included in this exhibition. They include: his connections to Abilene, the farmlands of Kansas and the myths of the Old West; his stature as a military hero, from his days in the West Point class of 1915 to his responsibilities as Supreme Allied Commander and five-star general in World War II; his reluctant candidacy for the presidency; his experiences as president of Columbia University; his transitional role as NATO Commander and his prominence as President of the United States. His hobbies achieved a stature seldom seen before, especially his love of golf and painting. Evident in many ways throughout the exhibition, the symbols of these events and experiences became a vital part of the realities and myths of Eisenhower's reputation.

This may be best illustrated in several distinctive objects included in the exhibition. Not master paintings or sculpture, they are instead articles of attire, worn by the president and his first lady. One is a unique dress, tailored especially for Mamie, from a custom-designed Schumacher fabric originally intended for decorative use in the renovation of Blair House. This fabric, manufactured in a variety of colors, included images of the prime residences and architectural landmarks of the Eisenhowers: the Abilene house, West Point, Mamie's childhood home in Denver, Columbia University, the Gettysburg House and the White House. Clustered around these architectural references are a related system of symbols: the presidential seal, the five stars of the general, the Republican elephant, flags and weapons, the SHAEF symbol within a shield from World War II and, perhaps surprisingly, a grouping of easels, paints and brushes. Deliberately planned and designed for historic references in the renovation of Blair House, this Schumacher fabric was obviously intended to embody the essence of the Eisenhower myth. So effective was the result that the first lady decided to have dresses designed and tailored using the material. She wore these dresses, and the historical messages they communicated, with great pride.

Eisenhower came to the presidency with his national and international reputation firmly established. The historical details of his life were widely known before he was sworn into office. As president, his legend continued to grow. The consistency of the officially codified iconography, as preserved in Mamie's printed fabric dress, and the public's less-structured interpretation of the legend, can be compared by examining a unique western shirt which was embroidered for Ike by Viola Grae. Like many

The Blair House fabric, designed by Dorothy Draper, includes images of residences, architectural landmarks and other symbols depicting the lives of Dwight and Mamie Eisenhower.

Left: This hand embroidered shirt by Viola Grae combines Ike's love of all things Western with icons of his life. Above: Handtooled boots again emphasize the "Ike icons."

of the paintings and objects presented in this exhibition, the loving details evident on this shirt reflect the tremendous affection of the public for the president. On it, several major symbols were repeated: the presidential seal, the five stars of the general and the Gettysburg house. Instead of the White House, the Capitol and the Washington Monument were shown. New symbols appeared: the longhorn and Kansas sunflower referred, as did the western shirt itself, to Ike's roots in Abilene and the Kansas of the Old West. The lone star and the bluebonnets represented the state of his birth, Texas. Also depicted were symbols of Ike's hobbies: fishing rods and hunting rifles on the cuffs, golf clubs and tees on the collars. A pair of handmade western boots, crafted in Texas, reinforce this imagery, including the presidential seal, the Capitol building, the Kansas sunflower and "Ike" stitched into the leather bootstraps.

When these details are viewed as a whole, they suggest the complexity and consistency of the iconography of Ike. While the president from Abilene may have been rooted in the 19th century, he participated quite actively in the dramatic evolutionary developments of the 20th century. As a politician, he realized that the challenges and technologies of the 21st century were approaching; yet many Americans were frightened by the implications of this change. Still stunned by the horrors of World War II and the destructive potential of the new technologies, many citizens retreated to the moral values and agrarian philosophies developed in the 19th century. They feared the uncertainties of the future. Eisenhower understood those fears and he certainly recognized the symbolic importance of those earlier values; they were the standards of his childhood in Abilene. As a result, the iconography of Ike centered on older, more stable values. His smile and his public image soothed the nation's fears and instilled a new sense of confidence.

Eisenhower was not only a shrewd and perceptive politician, he was also a five-star general and career military officer, the former Supreme Commander, who immediately grasped the military and defense implications of these powerful new technologies. Ever the politician, Eisenhower continually directed the nation's anxious gaze to Abilene and Gettysburg, where traditional small town virtues were embodied; to golf, fishing and painting; and to continuing family and business values. The age of the atomic bomb, the jet plane, space flight, television and advanced communications, though embraced by the man, remained isolated from the legend, the icon. While critics focused on his grin and his golf game, Eisenhower engineered the construction of a massive network of interstate highways designed to serve transportation and defense needs, opened the St. Lawrence Seaway, traveled the globe in jet craft and initiated the nation's space program.

A smiling elder statesman on the surface, he was, according to Murray Kempton a "great tortoise upon whose back the world sat," not realizing "the cunning beneath the shell."[52] Fully aware of Eisenhower's shrewdness, Richard Nixon indicated that "when it came to making a final decision, he was the coldest, most unemotional and analytic man in the world."[53] Of course, the public seldom glimpsed the private Eisenhower. The American public, and the world, saw the image of Ike, the dutiful soldier and reluctant president who seemed to prefer golf and painting to the formalities of the White House. The nation and the world trusted and respected Ike and Mamie during the 1950s. The nation prospered. Sons were not sacrificed on battlefields in remote lands. Americans liked Ike for good reason. They still do.

J. Richard Gruber

NOTES

1. Marquis Childs, *Eisenhower: Captive Hero, A Critical Study of the General, the President;* New York: Harcourt, Brace and Company, 1958, pp. 14–15.

2. Dwight D. Eisenhower, *At Ease: Stories I Tell to Friends,* New York: Doubleday and Company, Inc. 1967; reprinted by Eastern Acorn Press, 1989, p.65.

3. Stephen E. Ambrose, *Eisenhower, Volume One, Soldier, General of the Army, President-Elect, 1890–1952,* New York: Simon and Schuster, 1983, pp. 18–19.

4. Eisenhower, *At Ease,* p. 125.

5. Robert G. Athearn, *The Mythic West in Twentieth-Century America,* Foreword by Elliot West, Lawrence, Kansas: University Press of Kansas, 1986, p. 14.

6. See Neil Summers, *The First Official TV Western Book,* Vienna, W. VA: Old West Shop Publishing, 1987.

7. Ambrose, *Volume One,* p. 409.

8. Eisenhower, *At Ease,* p. 388.

9. Ambrose, *Volume One,* p. 412.

10. Ibid., p. 413.

11. Marquis W. Childs, "Why Ike Said No," *Collier's,* 122, August 28, 1948, p. 15.

12. Ibid., pp. 76–77.

13. Ambrose, *Volume One,* pp. 530–532.

14. Ralph M. Jennings, "Dramatic License in Political Broadcasts," *Journal of Broadcasting,* Vol. XII, No. 3, Summer 1968, p. 238.

15. Editors of *Broadcasting Magazine, The First Fifty Years of Broadcasting,* New York: Broadcasting Publications, 1982, p. 109.

16. Ibid., p. 132.

17. Ibid., p. 109.

18. Ibid., p. 109.

19. Ambrose, *Volume One,* pp. 550–553.

20. Ibid., 571.

21. Sidney Hyman, "Absorbing Study of Popularity," *The New York Times Magazine,* July 24, 1960, pp. 7, 24–25.

22. Childs, *Eisenhower: Captive Hero,* p. 186.

23. Robert Wright, "eisenhower's fifties," *Antioch Review,* Vol. 38, Summer 1980, pp. 280–81.

24. Lance Morrow, "Dreaming of the Eisenhower Years," *Time,* Vol. 116, July 28, 1980, p. 32.

25. Murray Kempton, "The Underestimation of Dwight D. Eisenhower," *Esquire,* Vol. 68, September 1967, p. 156.

26. Richard Rhodes, "Ike: An Artist In Iron," *Harper's Magazine,* July 1970, pp. 72–76.

27. Fred I. Greenstein, "Eisenhower as an Activist President: A Look at New Evidence," *Political Science Quarterly,* Vol. 94 No. 4, Winter 1979–80, p. 577.

28. Arthur Schlesinger, Jr., "The Eisenhower Presidency: A Reassessment," *Look,* May 14, 1979, p. 42.

29. Morrow, "Dreaming of the Eisenhower Years," p. 32.

30. Stephen E. Ambrose, *Eisenhower, Volume Two, The President,* New York: Simon and Schuster, 1984, pp. 16–18.

31. Ibid., pp. 26–27.

32. Ibid., p. 370.

33. Jennings, "Dramatic License in Political Broadcasts," p. 241.

34. Kenneth S. Davis, *The Eisenhower College Collection, The Paintings of Dwight David Eisenhower,* Los Angeles: Nash Publishing, 1972, p. 149.

35. Ibid., p. 149.

36. Eisenhower, *At Ease,* p. 341.

37. Ibid., p. 341.

38. Ibid., p. 341.

39.Ambrose, *Volume Two,* p. 392.

40. Ibid., p. 74.

41. Ibid., p. 28.

42. Ibid., p. 96. (Also see Stan Cohen, *The Eisenhowers, Gettysburg's First Family,* Charleston, West Virginia: Pictorial Histories Publishing Company, 1986, pp. 26–27.

43. Lois Gordon and Alan Gordon, *American Chronicle, Six Decades in American Life, 1920-1980,* New York: Atheneum, 1987, pp. 342–350.

44. John Patrick Diggins, *The Proud Decades, America in War and in Peace, 1941–1960,* New York: W.W. Norton and Company, 1989, pp. 182–183.

45. Ibid., p.184. See also Chester H. Liebs, *Main Street to Miracle Mile, American Roadside Architecture,* Boston: Little, Brown and Company, 1985; J. Richard Gruber, "Interview with Kemmons Wilson" in *Memphis 1948–1958,* Memphis: Memphis Brooks Museum of Art, 1986, pp. 128–133.

46. Lois Gordon and Alan Gordon, *American Chronicle,* p. 360.

47. Richard Horn, *Fifties Style, Then and Now,* New York: Beech Tree Books, 1985, p. 158.

48. See Lois Gordon and Alan Gordon, *American Chronicle,* pp. 326–327, 334–336, 344–345.

49. Peter Guralnick, "Elvis Presley," in *The Rolling Stone Illustrated History of Rock and Roll,* Edited by Jim Miller, New York: Random House/Rolling Stone Press, 1980, pp. 19–34.

50. For a consideration of the cultural significance of these years, see J. Meredith Neil, "1955: The Beginning of Our Own Times," *South Atlantic Quarterly,* Vol. 73, Autumn 1974, pp. 428–44.

51. Lois Gordon and Alan Gordon, *American Chronicle,* p. 390.

52. Murray Kempton, "The Underestimation of Dwight D. Eisenhower," p. 156.

53. Richard Rhodes, "Ike: An Artist In Iron," p. 72.

The entire nation loved Mamie and Ike for the grace,
prosperity, peace and vitality they brought to America
in the 1950s.

IKE: THE CAMPAIGNER

Left: Dwight D. Eisenhower at the 1952 Republican convention.
Above: His image as national and international hero of World War II made his
path to the White House almost inevitable.

QUESTION BY ADLAI STEVENSON'S CAMPAIGN MANAGERS:

"We tried the 'eggheads' once.
Besides, where else can they go?"

—Washington Post, Sept. 16, 1956

ANSWER FROM CASE, COMMITTEE OF ARTS & SCIENCES:

The 'Eggheads' are going for Eisenhower

CASE the Committee of the Arts and Sciences for Eisenhower was organized in July, 1956, by a group of artists, scientists and educators. The organizers of CASE and the many hundreds of members who have since joined are unified in their endorsement of President Eisenhower's leadership and the major achievements and goals of his program.

Because the men and women of CASE are thoughtful and intellectually independent men and women, they have many and individually varying reasons for their support of the President. It is this very independence and variety of thought that makes their backing doubly welcome to a President who has the greatest respect for the scientific and cultural achievements of his fellow citizens.

The organizing members of CASE are in agreement on certain compelling general reasons for their endorsement of President Eisenhower:

1. **Science and culture can flourish only in a world at peace.** Dwight D. Eisenhower as President has proved to the people of America and of the world that he represents an effective force for attaining and preserving *"freedom and justice and peace for all peoples."*

2. **Artists, scientists and educators have everything to gain from a stable economy and almost everything to lose from an unstable one.** The Eisenhower Administration has successfully stood for stabilizing the value of the dollar in a period of peacetime prosperity, while avoiding interference by government control. As the result of enlightened economic policies developed with the advice of scholars, the record of the first four years of the Eisenhower Administration has been unparalleled in American history. With it has come self-sufficiency for more artists, scientists and educators than ever before. The further progress of the arts, science and education depends upon the continuation of a sound economy. As the President has said, *"America does not prosper unless all Americans prosper."*

3. **Scientific, scholastic and artistic achievements are largely the achievements of individual enterprise and genius.** President Eisenhower has recognized this by deed and word. He believes that the sanctity and dignity of the individual lie at the heart of representative government and that personal freedom in thought and action is essential to creative effort for the betterment of all mankind. In his own words, *"The individual is of supreme importance."*

DEAN HARRY J. CARMAN Co-Chairmen HELEN HAYES

DR. HOWARD HANSON
Chairman, Arts Branch
DR. JAMES PHINNEY BAXTER III
Chairman, Education Branch
VERA WARDNER DOUGAN
Chairman, Music Division
ANDREW WYETH & FELIX DE WELDON
Co-Chairmen, Art & Architecture Div.

DR. ROGER ADAMS
Chairman, Science Branch
J. DONALD ADAMS
Chairman, Literary Division
ROBERT MONTGOMERY & IRENE DUNNE
Co-Chairmen, Entertainment Arts Div.
M. ROBERT ROGERS
Executive Director

Advisory Board:
MRS. JOUETT SHOUSE (chairman), DR. DETLEV BRONK, ADM. RICHARD E. BYRD, DR. LAURENCE GOULD, PROF. MALCOLM MOOS, EUGENE ORMANDY, PORTIA WASHINGTON PITTMAN.

CASE 1406 G STREET N.W., WASH. 5, D.C.
Committee of the Arts and Sciences for Eisenhower

A PARTIAL LISTING OF MEMBERS
Members' Affiliations Are Listed for Identification Only and Do Not Signify an Endorsement by Their Institutions

ART AND ARCHITECTURE · EDUCATION · ENTERTAINMENT ARTS · LITERATURE · MUSIC · SCIENCE

We Regret That Space Limitations Require Omission of Several Hundred Names

If anything, Ike was even more popular in 1956 than 1952. Former Stevenson supporters backed Eisenhower, guaranteeing a landslide victory.

The plethora of campaign materials
from Ike's 1952 and 1956 campaigns
are still classic examples of graphic
design, advertising, imaging and
political statement.

Gadgets, memorabilia, wearable
campaign items all made a bold
political statement.

A master of both old and new forms of politicking. Eisenhower used the old fashioned whistle stop campaign as ably as he did television and mass media.

Eisenhower—the man who was born in the cattle town of Abilene—led America into the New Frontier with the start of the space program following Russia's launching of the Sputnik in 1957. Here, in 1960, Eisenhower views the rapid progress of America in the space race at Huntsville, Alabama's Marshall Space Center.

IKE: THE PRESIDENT

Truman and Eisenhower on the way to Inauguration ceremonies.

Above: The presidential jet, the Columbine, was named for the state flower of Mamie's home state of Colorado. Ike satisfied his lust for travel in a whirlwind flight to 18 countries in 11 days during his second term.

Right: One of the easier presidential duties for an active man like Ike—throwing out the first ball in the 1954 baseball season.

Eisenhower addressing the United
Nations in his "Atoms for Peace"
speech December, 1953.

The President awards a medal to a Korean War nurse at the White House, 1954.

Anne and David Eisenhower, Julie and Tricia Nixon join the President and Vice President at 1957 Inauguration Parade.

Above: The Nixons and Eisenhowers ready for a formal affair.

Left: President and Mrs. Eisenhower welcome His Excellency Haile Selassie and wife to the White House.

Left: September 9, 1957 Eisenhower signs landmark civil rights legislation.

Below: In a scene straight out of a 1950s era sci-fi movie, Eisenhower gives a "scientific talk" with visual aid.

Left: Eisenhower welcomes King Faisal of Saudia Arabia in September, 1957.

Below: One of our most well traveled presidents, Eisenhower prepares to board a helicopter on the White House lawn.

In his youth in Abilene, President Eisenhower read and heard about the Old Frontier of the West. During his presidency he expanded the frontiers of the United States by being the first and, to date, only president to admit areas to the Union which were not a part of the continental United States and by beginning the space program, which gave our frontiers yet another dimension.

Eisenhower is shown here on January 3, 1959 signing legislation admitting Alaska as the 49th state, and seven months later, on August 21, 1959, admitting Hawaii as the 50th state in the United States of America.

Mamie Eisenhower and 1959 Easter Seal Child Phillip Little.

Two heros meet: Dwight Eisenhower and John Wayne at a congressional dinner.

Right: June 26, 1959. President Eisenhower and Queen Elizabeth participate in dedication ceremonies for the St. Lawrence Seaway.

Below: Dwight Eisenhower and Nikita Khruschev in front of Aspen Lodge, Camp David.

John Foster Dulles, Winston Churchill,
Dwight Eisenhower and Anthony Eden
relaxing at the White House.

Charles DeGaulle, Prime Minister of
France, and President Eisenhower in
April, 1960 motorcade.

August, 1960. Eisenhower announces
successful launching of the Discoverer
XIII Satellite.

Jackie Kennedy and Mamie Eisenhower
in front of the White House, December
1960.

This watercolor by Chester Bratten was
used by the Green Cross and the
Advertising Council for a campaign for
safe driving.

This oil painting by Charlotte Joan
Sternberg was completed in 1961,
shortly after Eisenhower left office.

Ike was an artist: an artist at relaxing,
at speaking, at working with people,
and in his own private studio.

IKE: AT EASE

Friends, family, photographs and memory were all subjects for Ike's brush—his "daubs" as he rather modestly called them.

Eisenhower Family Home, n.d.,
Collection of the Dwight D. Eisenhower
Library, gift of the Estate of Kevin
McCann.

Ike, after he took up painting, always
had one room in each residence for his
artist's studio.

Portion of the Seine River, 1951, Collection of the Dwight D. Eisenhower Library, gift of Brig. Gen. and Mrs. Edwin B. Howard.

Snowcapped Mountains, n.d., Collection of the Dwight D. Eisenhower Library, gift of the Estate of Thomas E. Stephens.

Deserted Barn, 1959, Collection of the Dwight D. Eisenhower Library, gift of Dwight D. Eisenhower.

Abraham Lincoln, 1935, Collection of the Dwight D. Eisenhower Library, gift of Dwight D. Eisenhower.

George Washington, n.d., Collection of the Dwight D. Eisenhower Library, gift of Dwight D. Eisenhower.

Floyd Odlum, 1955, Collection of the Dwight D. Eisenhower Library, gift of the Estate of Floyd Odlum.

Princess Anne, 1957, Collection of the Dwight D. Eisenhower Library, gift of Howard Young.

Secretary of State–John Foster Dulles
Secretary of Treasury–George M. Humphrey
Secretary of Defense–George E. Wilson
Collection of the Dwight D. Eisenhower Library, gift of Dwight D. Eisenhower.

Another passion was golfing, which he did as often as time permitted, even constructing a putting green outside the White House and his Gettysburg house.

Bridge was Ike's favorite card game.

Below: Ike gives some pointers to David Eisenhower. The President's longtime valet and friend John Moaney looks on.

Playing Scrabble at Camp David—like other Americans, the Eisenhowers participated in fads of the 50s.

Always a Kansas farm boy at heart, Ike is shown here inspecting one of his black angus cattle.

Above: Fishing was another popular relaxation for Ike, the outdoorsman.

Left: Skeet shooting with friends.

After dinner with the grandchildren at Gettysburg, September 1956.

Christmas Day, 1953. Ike is caught trying out his new Christmas present on another photographer.

Dwight and Mamie at the Gettysburg
farm, September 1956.

W E L I K E I K E

Above: This Bas Relief wood carving of Eisenhower was a gift from Carlos P. Garcia of Manila in June of 1958.

Opposite page: This oil painting on black velvet of Ike was done by the concessionaire at Clark Air Force Base, Phillipines in 1958.

An admirer from Mexico made this silk thread tapestry portrait of Ike.

Two wood carvings, both approximately 8" high, of Eisenhower. The one on the left was made in Michigan, and the other is from Sweden.

M. Rais Khan of Pakistan drew this image of Eisenhower on a large translucent tree leaf. The leaf is sandwiched between two pieces of glass.

A needlework picture of Ike with his portrait surrounded by various icons, including the Republican elephant and the White House.

Opposite page: This batik shows Eisenhower cooking up a batch of his famous chili.

Below: This porcelain figure of Mamie Doud Eisenhower wearing her first Inaugural gown. 12" high.

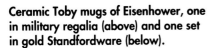

Ceramic Toby mugs of Eisenhower, one in military regalia (above) and one set in gold Standfordware (below).

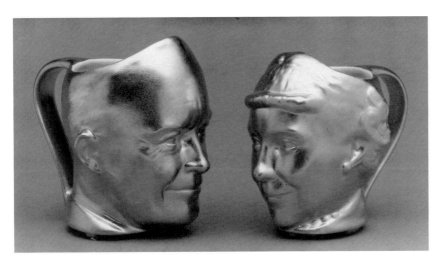

Opposite page: A collage by Mr. Georges Renier of France consists of cut-up postage stamps forming a bust of Eisenhower in civilian garb.

Right: A double picture of Eisenhower (top) and Adlai Stevenson (bottom) painted on vertical wood slats in 1956.

Below: Beadwork given to Eisenhower on a visit to India from the Children's Museum Foundation, Amreil, India.

All the presidents from Washington to Truman are standing in front of the White House with a bust portrait of Eisenhower above the door. This 3 $\frac{1}{2}$' x 7 $\frac{1}{2}$' painting was done by J.B. McCoy of Ohio.

Above: Decorations on this felt poodle skirt include symbols of "Atoms for Peace," "Equal Rights" and "Full Employment." Worn during the 1956 election.

Right: Ike models a western shirt with embroidery depicting his life and accomplishments.

Handtooled boots made for Eisenhower include many icons of his life.

Below:
Amon Carter of Ft. Worth, Texas presented this set of six-shooters to Eisenhower in 1945.

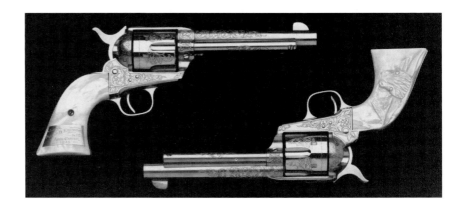

Bob Wygart of Houston, Texas did this oil painting of Ike in a grey Western Hat.

Below: "The Man from Abilene," painted by Louis Tepper, shows Ike dressed in Western clothes and riding a Pinto horse.

THE IKE YEARS
1952-1960

1952

Quote of the year:
"And you know the kids love that dog [Checkers] and I just want to say this right now, that regardless of what they say about it, we're going to keep it."
Richard Nixon in his Checkers speech

Lucille Ball makes TV history when she appears pregnant on *I Love Lucy*

Jackson Pollock's *Number 12, Convergence* is completed. Willem de Kooning paints *Woman I* and *Woman II*

General Fulgencio Batista ousts elected leaders in Cuba

Ernest Hemingway wins Pulitzer Prize for *The Old Man and the Sea*

Jonas Salk, 38, tests his vaccine against polio at the University of Pittsburgh; a polio epidemic strikes more than 50,000

Clyde Lovellette of the University of Kansas is named Player of the Year in college basketball; KU wins college basketball championship title

The nation's first Holiday Inn opens in Memphis, Tennessee

George Jorgensen, 26, is surgically transformed into a woman (Christine) in Denmark

Lillian Hellman, testifying before the House states "I cannot and will not cut my conscience to fit this year's fashions."

The American Ballet Center is founded by Robert Joffrey

The first plastic artificial heart valve is used on a patient at the Georgetown Medical Center

TV premieres include *The Jackie Gleason Show*, *Death Valley Days*, *Dragnet*, and *The Adventures of Ozzie and Harriet*

New York beats Brooklyn in seven games in World Series

Subversives are barred from teaching in public schools

Ray Kroc begins franchising McDonald's

Nehru is elected Prime Minister in India's first national election

U.S. explodes hydrogen bomb on Entiwetok Atoll on November 1

The Greatest Show On Earth wins the Academy Award for Best Picture

Modern Jazz Quartet is organized

Bwana Devil, the first full-length 3-D film, premiered on November 26, 1952, in Los Angeles, initiating a new film fad

In July, the Republican National Convention in Chicago becomes the first national political convention to be covered by live TV; Dwight Eisenhower is the Republican nominee

November 4, Eisenhower elected: 33,936,234 votes (55.1%) to Stevenson's 27,214,992 votes (44.1%)

In fashion, "Mamie bangs" are becoming popular; the "poodle" cut and ponytails also increasingly prevalent

Lever House, designed by Gordon Bunshaft of Skidmore, Owings & Merrill, opens in New York

Harry Bertoia's Diamond chair, fabricated of welded steel lattice work, is first introduced by Knoll

New in 1952: Cinerama, Sony transistor radio, Kellogg Sugar Frosted Flakes, Weber Kettle Grill (designed by George Stephen), mechanical lawn mowers, 16mm home movie projectors, Ray-Ban Wayfarer sunglasses (designed by Ray Stegeman)

1953

Quote of the Year:
"What was good for our country was good for General Motors and vice versa."
Secretary of Defense Charles Wilson

January 20, Eisenhower inauguration, largest inaugural crowd in U.S. history

Elizabeth II is crowned Queen of England

Edmund Hillary and Sherpa Tenzing Norkay scale Mt. Everest

Joseph Stalin dies at 72, Georgi Malenkov becomes Soviet Premier

Sergei Prokofiev, Queen Mary, and Eugene O'Neill die

1954

Quote of the Year:
"The doctrine of 'separate but equal' has no place [in public education]...Separate facilities are inherently unequal."
Supreme Court Decision, *Brown v. Board of Education of Topeka*

Dag Hammarskjold is elected UN Secretary General

Department of Health, Education and Welfare is created

"The smart woman will keep herself desirable. It is her duty to be feminine and desirable at all times in the eyes of the opposite sex." Leland Kirdel, Coronet

Elvis Presley pays $4.00 to cut *My Happiness* for his mother's birthday

Glenn Miller is top performer of the year

Picnic by William Inge wins Pulitzer Prize

Charles Yaeger goes a record 1,600 mph in a Bell X-1A at Edwards AFB, California

Sexual Behavior in the Human Female by Alfred C. Kinsey hits the bestseller lists

The Salk Vaccine is certified to prevent infantile paralysis

The first successful open heart surgery is performed at Jefferson Medical College, Philadelphia

Rocky Marciano knocks out Joe Walcott for the heavyweight title

Easter egg rolling is revived at the White House

Scrabble becomes a nationwide fad

30 million attend classical music performances; 15 million attend major league baseball

Ike's cabinet described as "eight millionaires and a plumber"

New TV programs include *You Are There*, *Person to Person*, *The Jack Paar Show*, *The Tonight Show*, *Make Room for Daddy* and *Soupy Sales*

General Motors introduces the Chevrolet Corvette, a plastic laminated fiberglass sports car; sells for $3,250

From Here to Eternity wins Academy Award for Best Picture

New in 1953: *TV Guide*; *Playboy*; IBM-701 (IBM's first computer); L&M cigarettes; Sugar Smacks

Eisenhower modifies the pledge of allegiance from "one nation indivisible" to "one nation, under God, indivisible."

The first atomic-powered submarine, USS Nautilus, is commissioned at Groton, Connecticut

Bubble prefab houses designed by architect Eliot Noyes become a craze in Hobe Sound, Florida

On the Waterfront sweeps Academy Awards for Best Picture, Best Director (Elia Kazan) and Best Actor (Marlon Brando)

Mississippi voters approve a constitutional amendment to abolish public schools if there is no other way to avoid segregation

Roger Bannister of England runs the mile in 3:59.4, the first under four minutes

The Tobacco Industry Research Committee reports there is "no proof...that cigarette smoking is a cause of lung cancer."

The Boeing 707, the first jet-powered transport, is tested

Hank Aaron, Milwaukee-NL debuts; Willie Mays wins batting title for the National League

Largest thermonuclear blast ever occurs at Bikini Atoll

Gamal Abdel Nasser becomes Premier of Egypt

The Pajama Game and *Peter Pan* are Broadway musical premieres

Maria Callas makes her American debut in Chicago, Chicago Lyric Opera, performing *Norma*

Armistice Day is changed to Veterans Day

Liberace becomes a TV sensation with his candelabra, soft lights and smile

Jimmy Durante's nose is injured as it is accidentally caught under Liberace's piano during a TV rehearsal

A record $3,135,000,000 is spent in new construction

Gas price is 29 cents a gallon

Elvis Presley makes his first commercial recording

Marilyn Monroe and Joe DiMaggio marry on January 14; they file for divorce on October 5

A Gallup Poll reports a family of four can live on $60 a week

Senate Hearings on Army—McCarthy dispute begin

French fortress at Dien Bien Phu, Vietnam, lost; total garrison is captured

The new Iwo Jima monument is dedicated in Washington, D.C.

Atomic Energy Commission denies security clearance to J. Robert Oppenheimer

British agree to return Suez Canal to Egypt in 1956

Pulitzer Prize for fiction awarded to William Faulkner for *A Fable*

Senate votes to condemn Joseph McCarthy for contempt of Senate

Alan Freed plays what he calls "rock 'n' roll" on radio station WINS

On December 15, 1954, Fess Parker portrays Davy Crockett on Walt Disney's TV show *Disneyland*, begins Davy Crockett and coonskin cap craze. Other popular new TV shows include: *Father Knows Best*, *The Jimmy Durante Show*, *People Are Funny*, *Lassie*, *The George Goebel Show*, *Stop The Music* and *The Loretta Young Show*

Formica's "Skylark" plastic laminate, designed by Nettie Hart, with boomerang pattern, achieves great popularity

New in 1954: frozen TV dinners, color television, Trix cereal, gas turbine automobile, Shakey's Pizza Parlor, F-100 Supersabre fighter

1955

Quote of the Year:
"Recognition of the Supreme Being is the first, the most basic, expression of Americanism. Without God, there could be no American form of government, nor American way of life."
Dwight D. Eisenhower

Winston Churchill resigns as Prime Minister of England

AFL and CIO merge, George Meany becomes president

Military ousts Juan Peron in Argentina

Bao Dai is ousted; South Vietnam proclaims republic

National Airlines fare from New York to Havana: $176.50 round trip

Malenkov is ousted for "deviation;" Khrushchev becomes Party Secretary in Soviet Union

East of Eden, Rebel Without a Cause are hit movies; James Dean, 24, dies in car crash on September 30

Eddie Fisher and Debbie Reynolds form what fan magazines call "the perfect union"

The Honeymooners goes on the air and ends after 39 episodes

Cannonball Adderly makes his first recording

Cat on a Hot Tin Roof opens on Broadway and wins Tennessee Williams a Pulitzer

$17 million Walt Disney Amusement Park in Anaheim is under construction

An oral contraceptive made of progesterone-type substance is discovered by Gregory Pincus

The AEC reports that fallout from last year's H-bomb tests at Bikini will affect human life in a 7,000 square mile area

Sugar Ray Robinson comes out of retirement to knock out Bobo Olson and win the middleweight title for the third time

Rock Around the Clock by Bill Haley and His Comets becomes major national hit

Junk mail enters the popular lexicon in America

The first TV presidential press conference with Eisenhower occurs January 19, 1955

Robert Rauschenberg creates *Bed*, which incorporates a real pillow and quilt on a stretcher, along with other objects and design materials; Jasper Johns creates *Target with Plaster Casts*

Smog becomes a public concern

Richard J. Daley becomes mayor of Chicago

Construction of suburban shopping centers and motels escalates

Carmen Miranda, Cordell Hull, Albert Einstein, Charlie Parker and Enrico Fermi die

Annie Oakley cowgirl outfit: $4.90

The first electric stove for home use is marketed

Minimum wage increases from 75 cents to $1

The Brooklyn Dodgers defeat The New York Yankees to win their first World Series

Edward Steichen assembles "The Family of Man" show at The Museum of Modern Art

Over 3.8 million Americans play golf on approximately 5,000 courses

Academy Award for Best Picture to *Marty*, also Best Director (Delbert Mann) and Best Actor (Ernest Borgnine)

Lawrence Ferlinghetti's City Lights Bookshop, in San Francisco, serves as a significant gathering place for major figures of the Beat Generation

TV's big quiz era initiated when Revlon buys *The $64,000 Question*. Other major new shows are: *Captain Kangaroo, The Lawrence Welk Show, The Honeymooners, The Mickey Mouse Club, Alfred Hitchcock Presents, The Millionaire* and *Gunsmoke*

Best selling books include *The Man in the Gray Flannel Suit, The Power of Positive Thinking* and *Andersonville*, which also wins MacKinlay Kantor the Pulitzer Prize for literature

In fashion the color pink is very popular; pink dress shirts become a fad for men

Architect Eero Saarinen's futuristic "Pedestal" tables and chairs introduced by Knoll

In September, Eisenhower suffers severe heart attack while staying in Denver; after six weeks in Denver hospital, he travels to Gettysburg farm to complete recuperation

New in 1955: Disneyland; *National Review; Village Voice;* Crest toothpaste; Ford Thunderbird; Nieman-Marcus in Houston; Gorton's Fish Sticks; H&R Block; roll-on deodorant; Chase Manhattan Bank

1956

Quote of the Year:
"Of all the accomplishments of the American woman, the one she brings off with the most spectacular success is having babies."
Life Magazine

Grace Kelly marries Prince Rainier of Monaco

11 blacks arrested during Montgomery bus boycott

Andrea Doria sinks after collision with *Stockholm*

Anti-Soviet demonstrations in Hungary; Russians retaliate

Playhouse 90 premieres with *Requiem for a Heavyweight*. Other new shows include: *Tic Tac Dough, Twenty-One, The Steve Allen Show, The Price is Right* and *NBC News— Huntley-Brinkley*

Don Larsen (New York, AL) pitches the first perfect game in a World Series

'Hillbilly singer" Elvis Presley debuts on "Stage Door," hosted by the Dorsey Brothers. Presley scores it big on the Hit Parade with four Top 10 songs: *Hound Dog, Love Me Tender, Heartbreak Hotel* and *Blue Suede Shoes*

The Diary of Anne Frank wins Tony & Pulitzer awards

Frank Lloyd Wright exhibits a design for a mile high skyscraper, 528 stories; construction begins on the Guggenheim Museum, another Wright design, in New York City

Techniques of hemodialysis, blood purification on an artificial kidney machine, are pioneered

The DNA molecule is photographed

The first American test rocket for sending a manmade satellite into orbit ascends 125 miles at 4,000 mph

Mickey Mantle & Hank Aaron win batting titles

Bill Russell, Boston, debuts in NBA after being named College Player of the Year

Ed Sullivan vows never to allow Elvis's performance on his TV show. He later pays Presley $50,000 for three appearances; the last is televised only from the waist up

Increasing numbers of people move to the suburbs

Marilyn Monroe and Arthur Miller marry on June 29

The ex-Mrs. Adlai Stevenson, Ellen Borden, announces she will vote for Eisenhower

17 recordings of *The Ballad of Davy Crockett* are made; Estes Kefauver campaigns in coonskin cap

The last Union veteran of the Civil War, Albert Woolson, dies

Drive-in theaters grow to over 7,000 in number

Only 17% of college-educated women work full time

Paul Hornung of Notre Dame wins Heisman Trophy

34% of high school graduates are entering college

Ford Motor Company goes public

"In God We Trust" as the motto of the United States is authorized

Jackson Pollock killed in automobile accident

Egypt and Israel clash, Gaza Strip falls to Israel; French and British land in Suez; Israel takes Sinai; U.S. emergency force is sent to Sinai

On November 6, voters elect Eisenhower to a second term; Eisenhower receives 35,581,003 votes, Stevenson receives 25,738,765. Eisenhower relies heavily on TV campaigning

Ngo Diem is elected president of South Vietnam

Around The World in Eighty Days wins Academy Award for Best Picture

Martin Luther King says: "Nonviolence is the most potent technique for oppressed people. Unearned suffering is redemptive"

John F. Kennedy is awarded Pulitzer Prize in biography for *Profiles in Courage*

The Charles Eames rosewood lounge chair and ottoman is introduced, soon become a design classic

Hawaiian shirts gain in popularity

Clairol ads ask "Does she or doesn't she?"

New in 1956: Pampers disposable diapers; Salem cigarettes; Betty Furness ads for Westinghouse; Imperial Margarine; Comet; Elvis Presley products

1957

Quote of the year:
"The first artificial earth satellite in the world...was successfully launched in the USSR..."
Tass, the Soviet news agency

Eisenhower inaugurated for second term as President

Sputnik I, the first space satellite, and Sputnik II, with dog Laika, are launched by Russians

The Ford Edsel is introduced

Unemployment at 4.3%

National Merit Scholarship program starts; 556 scholarship winners attend 160 colleges

Average annual salary: $4,230

Sophia Loren hits the scene as new sex goddess

Major John Glenn sets a new transcontinental record in a Navy BV-1P Voight Crusader — 3 hours, 23 minutes, 8.4 seconds

Jack Paar replaces Steve Allen on "The Tonight Show"

Jackie Robinson retires from baseball

Perry Mason, Wagon Train, Leave It To Beaver, American Bandstand are new TV shows

The Bridge on the River Kwai wins Academy Awards for Best Picture, Best Director (David Lean) and Best Actor (Alec Guinness)

West Side Story and *The Music Man* open on Broadway

Leonard Bernstein becomes Music Director of the New York Philharmonic

Carnegie Hall is scheduled to be razed on August 7

On The Road is published by Jack Kerouac; beat and beatnik become increasingly common terms

Darvon, a new pain killer, is marketed

Sugar Ray Robinson wins middleweight title for 4th time, beating Gene Fullmer

Wake Up Little Susie by the Everly Brothers is banned in Boston

Philip Morris, aware that its brown package will not sell on color TV, invests $250,000 to develop a colorful package

21 million people spend $2 billion on recreational fishing

Volkswagen sells 200,000 Beetles

Joseph McCarthy and Humphrey Bogart die

Arkansas National Guard blocks movement of black high school students in Little Rock; Eisenhower sends federal troops to Little Rock

U.S. satellite explodes at Cape Canaveral, Florida

Collier's magazine publishes last issue (after 38 years) on January 4, 1957

Video tape introduced; contributes to the decline of live television

Five of the top ten TV shows are westerns: *Gunsmoke, Tales of Wells Fargo, Have*

Gun-Will Travel, The Life and Legend of Wyatt Earp and *Restless Gun*

New in 1957: Ford convertible with retractable hard top; marketing of electric typewriter; Frisbee Flying Disc by Wham-O

1958

Quote of the Year:
"If the public wants to lower its standard of living by driving a cheap, crowded car, we'll make it."
Anonymous General Motors Exectutive

De Gaulle becomes the French Premiere

The first Pizza Hut opens in Wichita, Kansas at the corner of Kellogg and Bluff

Explorer I, the first U.S. satellite, is launched from Cape Canaveral

Pope Pius XII dies; Pope John XXIII is elected

The Frank Lloyd Wright - designed Guggenheim Museum opens

Boris Pasternak refuses Nobel Prize

Castro-led rebels seize provincial capital in Cuba

7 of the top 10 TV shows are Westerns, led by *Gunsmoke*. New shows include: *Concentration, The Donna Reed Show, Peter Gunn, Dr Joyce Brothers* and *77 Sunset Strip*

Stan Musial gets his 3,000th hit

A Turkey for the President starring Ronald Reagan and Nancy Davis, is shown on the GE Theater, Thanksgiving Day

Van Cliburn wins the first prize in the International Tchaikovsky Piano Competition

The first regular U.S. domestic jet service, from New York to Miami, begins

NASA is organized to unify and develop space efforts

Arnold Palmer is the top money-winner in the PGA with $42,607

Eleanor Roosevelt is the first person on the Most Admired Woman list for 11th year

Colorado and Kansas are overrun by grasshoppers

The construction of a nuclear power plant in California is stopped by court action of environmental groups

LA Dodger Roy Campanella fractures two back vertebrae and is paralyzed from the shoulders down

Treason charges against Ezra Pound are dropped because he is "not competent" to stand trial

Harvard tuition: $1,250

Blue jeans: $3.75

September 2, 1958, Eisenhower signs The National Cultural Center Act, leading to construction of Kennedy Center in Washington

Best-selling books include *Doctor Zhivago, Lolita, From The Terrace, Inside Russia Today, Aka-Aka* and *Kids Say The Darndest Things!*

Jasper Johns paints *Three Flags*; Louise Nevelson completes *Sky Cathedral*. Arne Jacobsen designs *Egg* chair

John Birch Society founded

Harry Truman blames recession on Eisenhower

Elvis Presley is inducted into Army on March 24

Wham-O company introduces $1.98 plastic rings it calls "Hula-Hoops"

Gigi wins Academy Awards for Best Picture and Best Director (Vicente Minnelli)

Brigitte Bardot becomes new sex symbol

United Arab Republic is formed by Syria and Egypt

Vice President Nixon is stoned in Caracas while on Goodwill Tour

Ike's chief aide, Sherman Adams, resigns over alleged bribe

Mies van der Rohe's designs for the Seagram Building (with Philip Johnson) and the Museum of Fine Arts, Houston, are completed

New in 1958: Integrated circuitry; stereo records, introduced by EMI and Decca;

Grammy Awards; Sweet 'n Low; American Express Card; Bank Americard; U.P.I.; Chevrolet Impala; Philco "Predicta" TV; National Defense Education Act

1959

Quote of the Year:
"I am not willing to accept the idea that there are no Communists left in this country. I think if we lift enough rocks we'll find some."
Sen. Barry Goldwater (R. Arizona)

Fidel Castro takes Havana; Batista flees

Mel Ott, Frank Lloyd Wright, Erroll Flynn die

Laos asks for US aid against North Vietnam aggression

Vince Lombardi becomes Green Bay coach

The Mercury Seven test pilots are selected by NASA

Nikita Khrushchev, in a visit to Des Moines says, "We have beaten you to the moon, but you have beaten us in sausage making."

Bonanza and the *Bell Telephone Hour* premier

George Reeves, star of *Superman*, commits suicide

Total of deaths from auto accidents in the United States surpasses the total of American deaths in war

Louis Leakey discovers 1.78 million year old skull

Wilt Chamberlain debuts in the National Basketball Association

A contaminated-cranberries scare around Thanksgiving frightens millions of Americans

Montreal Canadiens win their third straight Stanley Cup

1960

Quote of the Year:
"[We need] a new generation of leadership—new men to cope with new problems and new opportunities."
John F. Kennedy

The American Football League is formed by Lamar Hunt with 8 teams

Average car costs $1,180

Oklahoma repeals Prohibition

86% of the population owns a TV; the average person watches it 42 hours a week

Alaska is admitted to the Union as the 49th state

Hawaii is admitted as the 50th state

Eisenhower and Khrushchev meet at Camp David

Edward Teller, "father" of the H-bomb, says: "It is necessary to provide every person in the U.S. with a shelter." This advances growing bomb shelter construction movement

Buddy Holly, Ritchie Valens and The Big Bopper are killed in a plane crash

Modern art is declared duty free by a bill signed into law

Charles Van Doren admits his TV game show, *The $64,000 Question*, was fixed

Ben-Hur receives Academy Award for Best Picture, Best Director (William Wyler) and Best Actor (Charlton Heston)

Books on the best-seller list include *Hawaii, The Ugly American, Lady Chatterly's Lover, The Status Seekers* and *Charley Weaver's Letters from Mamma*

Ike completes 22,370 mile Goodwill Tour; welcomed in India as a "Prince of Peace"

Khrushchev is denied entrance to Disneyland

General Motors redesigns many of its cars; most grow even larger. Cadillac reaches new scale and standard of luxury, with pointed fins, vast new window areas, cruise control, air conditioning and power door locks

New in 1959: Domestic compact cars: the Falcon, the Lark; Barbie doll; a redesigned Lincoln penney; clear plastic bags for clothing

Princess Margaret and photographer Tony Armstrong-Jones marry

Isaac Stern leads campaign to save Carnegie Hall from destruction

South African police kill 92 blacks during demonstration at Sharpeville

The world's first weather satellite, Tiros I, is launched

Pete Rozelle becomes the first NFL commissioner

U-2 Reconnaisance jet, with pilot Gary Powers, is shot down over Russia; Powers is sentenced to 70 years in Moscow

John F. Kennedy wins Democratic nomination; Richard Nixon wins the GOP

Digital display for watches and pocket calculators invented

Cassius Clay wins Olympic Boxing Gold Medal in Summer Games. The US wins a gold for Ice Hockey in Winter Games

Peanuts, Li'l Abner and *Pogo* are most popular cartoons

Eisenhower summarizes the progress of his presidency as including a 15% increase in average family income, 20% in real wages, 25% in output of goods and more housing and school construction than ever before

Brooklyn singer Barbra Streisand wins a talent contest in a small Greenwich Village club

Ebbets Field is demolished for an apartment project

Lucille Ball and Desi Arnaz file for divorce

Ike postpones visit to Japan due to anti-American demonstrations

Belgian Congo becomes independent; U.N. forces sent to Congo

Khrushchev pounds shoe in anger at U.N.

Largest TV audience in history watches first Kennedy-Nixon debate

Jack Kennedy wins narrow election victory to become president

In fashion, Jackie Kennedy becomes the new model of style

To Kill a Mockingbird, by Harper Lee, wins Pulitzer Prize for fiction

National support of art is booming: numerous museums around the nation are under construction and art galleries are opening at an unprecedented pace

Andy Warhol, advancing Pop Art images, paints *Dick Tracy*

Academy Award for Best Picture in 1960 was awarded to *The Apartment*

Popular new TV shows include *My Three Sons, The Flintstones, Face The Nation, Route 66* and *Sing Along With Mitch*

New in 1960: Astroturf; aluminum cans for foods and beverages; felt-tip pens; Motown Records; Xerox 914 Copier; Ken dolls; the laser (created by Theodore Maiman)

NOTES

See *American Chronicle, Six Decades in American Life, 1920-1980*, by Lois Gordon and Alan Gordon, New York: Atheneum, 1987

The Proud Decades, America in War and in Peace, 1941-1960, by John Patrick Diggins, New York: W. W. Norton and Company, 1989

The First 50 Years of Broadcasting, by Editors of Broadcasting Magazine, New York: Broadcasting Publications, 1982

Memphis 1948-1958, by J. Richard Gruber, Memphis: Memphis Brooks Museum of Art, 1986

American Style, Classic Product Design from Airstream to Zippo, by Richard Sexton, San Francisco: Chronicle Books, 1987

Mid-Century Modern, Furniture of the 1950s by Cara Greenberg, New York: Harmony Books, 1984

BLAM! The Explosion of Pop, Minimalism, and Performance 1958-1964 by Barbara Haskell, New York: Whitney Museum of American Art, 1984